Investing for Beginners

The Fastest Way to Build Wealth in the Stock Market

Giovanni Rigters

Table of Contents

Introduction

If you want to know the proven methods of making money by investing, then you're in luck because I'm going to touch on the four different ways that you can make money in the stock market. I'm going to talk about mutual funds, index funds, ETFs, and more. Plus, I'm also going to talk about growth stocks versus income stocks and even more.

I will also touch on the difference between index funds and ETFs and how you can do the research to make sure that you invest in the correct fund. I'm going to reveal the four best index or ETF funds. And if you are planning on investing globally, I will highlight what you need to pay attention to.

I will also talk about the market cap and how that plays a role when you look at growth stocks and some of the indexes where you can find some of these growth stocks as well as giving my 2 cents on what I think of growth stocks.

We will then cover the best dividend stocks and the best dividend ETFs that you need to have on your watch list. After which, I will talk about the differences between the 401k, the IRA and the traditional brokerage account, and I'm going to touch on eight investing mistakes that investors make. So hopefully, you can avoid making the same mistakes.

You're an eager investor who's planning on making a lot of money in the stock market, but you need to know how to pick stocks. That's one thing that I will also delve into. I'm going to touch on the best stock that you need to have in your portfolio.

I'll also give you 5 tips on how to get rich by investing in the stock market. So, let's get started!

Chapter 1: 4 Ways to make money in the stock market

The stock market is still the easiest way to get rich. Now, it might not be the fastest, but if you think about it, by investing in the stock market, you can still build and maintain your wealth. You can create a passive income stream and you can also invest for your retirement because you don't, of course, want to work your whole life.

If you look at some of the billionaires that we know in today's day and age, billionaires such as Warren Buffett, Amancio Ortega, Carlos Slim, and even Bill Gates, they all have a good chunk of their wealth invested in the stock market, and they're pretty much just living off the proceeds and the dividends that they get from their investments.

Some companies that they invest in are Apple, Microsoft, and Coca-Cola. These are companies that you and I have access to invest in also, because these are publicly traded companies.

If you think about Warren Buffett. He made all his billions from investing in the stock market. It did not come from real estate. It did not come from crypto. It literally all came from investing in the stock market and buying companies. That's why I want to talk about the four different ways that you can make money by investing in the stock market.

A benefit of investing in the stock market is that it's extremely easy to get started investing in the stock market. It's even easier than getting into real estate or even starting your own business because all you need is a brokerage or an investment account and some money deposited in that account in order to get started.

Now, you don't even need that much money in your brokerage account because you don't have to buy a whole share or a bunch of stocks. You can literally buy a fraction of a share. Another benefit is that you can invest anywhere in the world as long as you have an Internet connection and you have access to your brokerage account or investment account.

Another benefit is that you are your own boss. You can decide what your investing style is so, if you're the type of investor that's more on the day trading side, buying and selling on a frequent basis, or you're more of an investor that likes to go after growth stocks, for example, stocks in the tech sector, or you're more of a value investor, a buy-and-hold investor. You can decide what type of investor you are, so you have control over your future.

And then the last benefit is that you have bragging rights. If you're the type of investor that likes to invest in individual companies, just like myself, let's say you bought Apple on Monday and then a week later, Apple goes up by 10% over the course of a week. You can go to your friends or family members and start bragging to them about your Apple stock. Of course, people will start asking you questions if they see that you're doing well with your investments.

Method #1 – Capital Gains
The first method to make money in the stock market is through capital gains. Now, the easiest one to understand is buy low, and sell high. So you buy a stock at a specific price and you sell it at a higher price. And the difference is your profit. Now, a stock, of course, represents ownership. So, whenever you're buying a stock, you own a piece of the company that you just bought, you're a shareholder or you're a stockholder.

Now, pay attention to those two words shares and stocks. When I first got introduced to the investing world, I had to figure out that despite them being used interchangeably, there is a difference.

A **share** is a single unit. A **stock** could be a single unit, or it could also be multiple units. So, you would say I own one share in Coke, or I own ten shares in Procter and Gamble. Or you could also say I own stock in Coca Cola and I own stock in Procter and Gamble. So, the best way to remember this is that you own shares of stock in a specific company.
Now, going back to capital gains, buy low, sell high. Let's say I bought one coke share at $55. A week later, it went up to $60 and I sell it. I just made a profit of five bucks. The words capital gain means my capital increased in value. It went from $55 to $60. So, I have a capital gain of five bucks. My capital gain is still something called unrealized if it's still trading in the market because when your investments are still in the stock market, they have the potential to go up, down or sideways.

Your capital gain, which is unrealized at the moment, becomes a realized capital gain when you sell your stock. So once your coke goes from $55 to $60, it's still an unrealized gain because it's still trading in the market. If I sell it at $60, it becomes a realized gain.

Method #2 – Short Selling

The second method of making money in the stock market is through short selling or selling short. Now, this is the opposite of buy low, sell high and this is more of a riskier technique. It's more of an advanced technique.

With short selling, you're selling high and buying low. And the difference is your profit. Let me explain with an example that's outside of the stock market. Then I'll bring it back to the stock market. Let's say your friend just bought the latest Playstation and you're having fun playing games on it. You're enjoying the games so much that you decide to ask him if you can borrow his Playstation from him. He decides to lend his PlayStation to you, but you're a horrible friend because you needed some money so you end up selling his PlayStation for $500 a day or two later.

Your friend reaches out to you and lets you know that he wants his Playstation back at the end of the week so he can play some games. You start to panic because you already sold the PlayStation and didn't know he would have wanted it back so fast.

You're visiting different stores, and you happen to go to one store that sells new PlayStations at $200.

Perfect, because you sold it for $500. You can buy it back for $200. So, you buy the new PlayStation for $200, you give it to your friend, and you just made a profit of $300 because you sold it at a high price of $500. You bought it back at $200. The difference, $300, that's your profit. That's the concept of short selling.

Bringing this concept to the stock market, when you short sell, your brokerage firm will potentially charge you some fees, and they will borrow those shares you are trying to sell from investors that are customers with your brokerage firm or outside of the company.

Now, the tricky thing about selling short is that it's a very risky method of making money in the stock market. At least with buy low, sell high, the only money that you can lose is the money that you have invested in the stock market.

So, let's say you invested $500 into the stock market in one company, and that company ends up going bankrupt. You're only out of that $500 that you invested, but with short selling, your losses could be unlimited.

So, for example, let's say you were participating in short selling and you made a short sale on Coca-Cola. Coca-Cola was trading at $55. You think that Coca-Cola is going to drop to $40 so you can buy it back and make a profit between $40 and $55, that's the profit that you're making, that $15.

But what ends up happening is that instead of Coca-Cola going down, the price goes up. So, from $55, it's not going down to $40. It's actually going to $60, $65, $70, $75. As you can see, your losses are going to be unlimited because you still have to buy back Coke and return those shares you borrowed.

Method #3 – Dividend Investing
The third way to make money in the stock market is through dividends. This is more of a passive income method of making money. Not all companies, but a lot of blue-chip companies, companies that are well established, might pay out a dividend.

Companies sell goods and services, and a portion of their profits also called their net income, are distributed to their shareholders in the form of a dividend. This is also one of my favorite ways of making money in the stock market, and I have my own rules on analyzing specific companies to see how they pay their dividend and if they're increasing the dividend because something that's extremely important to me is that companies that do pay a dividend, need to be consistent with the dividends that they pay and the dividend payment needs to grow faster than inflation year over year. That's a requirement that I have for these companies.

Method #4 – Options Trading
The fourth method to make money in the stock market is through options trading. Now, options trading can get a little bit confusing, but I'll explain it in a way that's easy to understand by talking about the **call option** method.

Let's say you own 100 shares of stock in Coke. You bought Coke for $55. You're making money from Coke because Coke pays dividends. They pay a dividend every quarter. So, every quarter you get dividend payments, but you're not satisfied.

You want to make even more money from your shares of stock in Coke. So, you end up writing an options contract. In that contract, you state that you're willing to sell your 100 shares of Coke at $60, $60 is also called the **strike price**. The reason why I say

100 shares of stock is because the options contract is usually a lot of 100 shares.

Now, if the buyer of this option contract agrees with your contract, he must pay you a **premium**. Now, a premium might be $1 per share on this options contract for my 100 shares in Coke.

Now, the premium could be influenced by a multitude of things. If the options contract is for a stock that is popular, then it's going to have an impact on the value of the premium. The closer the actual price of the stock is to the strike price, that means that the premium is usually going to be higher.

But let's stick with one buck for one share in Coke, and an options contract is a lot of 100. So, we're getting a premium of $100 directly deposited into our brokerage account.

Let's talk about how the seller is making money. In this case, if Coke, which I bought for 55 bucks, never went up to the strike price, more than likely, the buyer is not going to execute the option because why execute the options contract on Coke when it's trading below 60? So, I just made some additional money without even selling my shares in coke because I still own the shares, and I made a quick 100 bucks. Now, even if the options contract did get executed, I would still make some money because I bought it at 55, and then the stock went up to 60, and it might even end up trading above 60.

The options contract gets executed and the buyer buys my 100 shares at $60. I still made a profit of $500, plus the additional 100 bucks because I bought it at 55, it went up to $60. So that's a $5 increase. I own 100 shares in Coke, so five times 100. I made a profit of $500 plus the premium of $100. So, I just made a total profit of $600.

If we look at this contract from the buyer's side. I'm already $100 in the hole because I had to pay that as a premium to the seller. Now, if Coke never goes up to 60, I'm not going to execute that option because why buy Coke at 60 when it's trading under 60? But here's the cool thing. If Coke goes up from 55 to 60, I execute the trade, and it ends up going to 65. Now, I just potentially made $400 in profit.

Coke went from 55 to 60. I execute the trade as the buyer and then it goes from 60 to 65. Now, I just made a $5 profit per share and I own 100 shares, so that's 500 bucks. It's still an unrealized gain, of course, and I end up selling at 65. I just made a quick profit of 400 bucks, because that 500 bucks minus the premium of $100 gives me that $400 in profit. That's pretty much how you want to look at options trading simplified.

Bonus Method

There is a bonus method that I want to mention when it comes to making some additional income with the stocks that you already own. This is a passive income method besides investing in dividend-paying stocks.

This method is called stock lending. You lend out the stocks that you own, for example, to investors who want to participate in short selling. Now, you do want to be careful with this method because if you own stocks that do pay a dividend, you want to make sure that you still get the dividend payment.

Also, if you're lending out your stock, every brokerage firm is a little bit different. So double-check with your brokerage firm and make sure that you aren't taxed in a different manner when it comes to this method. For example, with Robinhood, you can sign up for stock lending. But make sure that you double-check the fine print on stock lending. Now, this will not make you a millionaire, but it is a quick way to make some additional passive income.

Chapter 2: Index funds vs Mutual Funds vs ETFs

Let's dive in and talk about investing in mutual funds, ETFs, index funds, and even bonds. What are these funds? Actually, the best way to look at them and to think about them is that you have a pool of different investors' money. That money gets invested into different securities by a fund or money manager, different securities such as stocks, bonds, commodities, etc., or even a combination of those.

Now the benefit of this is that you might be an investor that does not want to invest in an individual stock, but you need something that's a little bit safer or maybe a bit more diversified. That's where these funds play a major role in your investment accounts.

When you invest in individual stocks, it's extremely exciting because it's high risk, high reward. So, you can see your stocks shoot up to the moon, but you can also easily see them come crashing down. A lot of investors cannot stomach seeing their investment portfolio drop by 30%, or even 40%. And if you think about it, when you invest in individual stocks, there's a lot of research that needs to be done and a lot of analysis, also called **fundamental analysis**. This is where you look at the financial metrics of a company to see how profitable that company is. So, you might look at the **net income** that a company generates, the **return on invested capital**, the **return on equity**, the **gross profits**, etc.

Advantages of investing in Funds

Investing in specific funds gives you immediate diversification. That's one of the benefits compared to investing in individual stocks. So, let's say you invest in an ETF, also called an exchange-traded fund, which invests in different companies in the tech sector. You have immediate diversification in tech stocks, which you don't have when you invest in individual companies. Or you have an index fund that invests in the companies that are in the S&P 500, you have that immediate diversification.

Another benefit is that index funds, mutual funds, and even ETF investing are a passive way of investing. When you have to analyze stocks, you're actively doing research and analyzing these companies. But investing in a fund, it's a more passive way of investing because you have your hard-earned money that you just put into your brokerage account and at the right time, you buy shares in an ETF, index fund, mutual fund, etc.

Also, another benefit of investing in a fund is that the research has already been done for you and the research is still being done by the fund manager to make sure that the correct companies are in the fund that you're invested in. This makes it extremely easy because all you must do is make sure that you're investing in the right fund based on your investing needs. In order to get that confidence, to know that you're investing in the correct fund, you need to look at the track record and the history of how that fund has performed. This will give you the confidence to make sure that that fund will potentially perform well in the future.

The future is always unpredictable, and anything can happen. But looking at history and also looking at the fund managers' performance will give you the confidence to make sure that this is the fund that you want to invest in for the long term. Questions that you need to ask yourself: how long has the fund manager been in the business? How many different funds is he or she managing?

Disadvantages of Fund investing
Some of the disadvantages of investing in a fund is that you're pretty much taking your hard-earned money, and you're giving it to a fund manager, and

you're telling the fund manager: here, go ahead, take my money, and invest it.

And for that privilege, you will pay the fund manager a fee. Some investors don't like this setup. They still like to be hands-on with their investments and would rather trade with individual companies, day trade, swing trade, etc.

Another disadvantage of investing in a fund is that you might not pay attention to what you're actually investing in. There's always a list of companies that you will be invested in, but you might not see that full list upfront. If you are morally against specific businesses or business practices, let's say you don't like weapon manufacturing or sales, or you don't like for-profit prison systems, or you're against CBD, then you want to make sure that the fund that you're investing in is not invested in these types of companies.

Nowadays, with technology, it's pretty easy to get a full list of the companies in a specific fund because all you have to do is go to the company's website, get a full list of the companies in the fund, or you can even request it from the funds' website.

You could also go to the SEC website and put in the **ticker symbol** of the fund and get a list of all the companies in that specific fund.

Even when I look at my investing strategy, I love investing in individual companies. I like doing research and putting them on my watch list that I keep an eye on, and I buy them whenever they're selling at a discount, whenever the value is there. Preferably dividend-paying companies. But I also have different funds that I invest in, such as different ETFs and index funds, and it makes my portfolio balanced. Because there's instant diversification when I invest in these ETFs and index funds. But then I also have the individual stocks where I'm making some passive income through my dividend-paying stocks.

Index Funds/ETFs vs Mutual Funds

Why do index funds and ETFs reign supreme over mutual funds on average? It's because of two things: the fees and the performance. Let's look at the fees first, and whenever I'm talking about the fees, I'm specifically talking about the **expense ratio**. Now, the expense ratio can cover various fees such as administrative fees, operating costs, commissions, advertising, etc. These are fees that you will have to pay as an investor if you invest in a fund.

On average, a mutual fund has a much higher fee and expense ratio than an index fund or an ETF that you're investing in. Mutual funds are actively managed by the fund manager, which means that the fund manager does all the research, the buying, and the selling of all the securities in that specific fund and all the fees associated with the buying, selling, administrative costs, etc. Even paying the fund manager's bonus that's all being paid by you.

Now with an index fund or an ETF, those usually track an underlying asset. For example, if you're investing in an index fund that tracks all the companies in the **S&P 500**, the fee is going to be a lot lower because all that fund does is mirror all the companies in the S&P 500. When you look at a mutual fund, you can easily see fees in the 1% or even higher. But with an index fund, you can see fees that are 0.1% or even lower. And yes, even if a fund performs well (your fund went up 8% in a year, or maybe even 10%). You would still have to consider your expense ratio fees into your capital gain.

The second reason is performance. It has been noticed that mutual funds, in the short term, are able to outperform index funds and ETFs. But in the long term, index funds and ETFs that are being used as the benchmark have widely outperformed mutual funds. And then, with mutual funds, you still have to add on that high expense ratio.

Bond Investing

To explain bond investing, all you must understand is that you're lending out your money and you're getting interest payments back and at the end of a specific period, you get your invested capital back.

So, a corporation could go the stock market route to get money and make an **initial public offering,** or they could also go the loan route, same with a governmental institution. So, with a governmental institution, you lend your money to them, which is your capital, and they will tell you that they owe you. So, they're getting your capital and while having it in their possession, they will spend it on fixing roads, building infrastructure, libraries, etc. They're then going to give you interest payments on a frequent basis, once every six months. And then they're going to give you your invested capital back at a specific date, also called the **maturity date**. And some of the bonds that you can invest in are going to be your **corporate bonds, governmental bonds, municipal**

bonds, which are going to be your local government, and the list goes on.

I like investing in a **bond fund**, because when you invest in one, you don't have to do the research on which bonds to invest in because it is exciting to invest in individual stocks as you're doing the research and you have the hope that the stock that you're investing in is going to shoot to the moon and make you a lot of money.

But with bond investing, it's a lot more stable. It's a lot more risk-averse. It's more of a fixed-income asset. So it's a lot more boring when it comes to investing in bonds. I like bond funds, because I use them as a way to make **passive income** on a monthly basis. I get my interest payments from my bond fund. Now, if you invest in individual bonds, you get paid every six months, but with a bond fund, because the bond fund is invested in so many different bonds and some of those are hitting the maturity date, some of those are hitting an interest payment date.
So, you're constantly getting paid interest on a monthly basis. And then also, if you invest in individual bonds, there will be a maturity date when you will get your invested capital back. Then you must

take that capital again and then invest it in another bond.

But when you invest in a bond fund, you will never have to worry about that because some of the bonds mature and then the fund manager is already investing in more recent bonds. So, you can just hold on to your bond fund and use it as a passive income stream.

Chapter 3: 4 best Index Funds (ETFs)

An index fund or an ETF is nothing more than a collection of securities that mirror a specific investment portfolio. So, for example, if you take the S&P 500, which is an index of the 500 biggest companies in the US, those companies within that investment have their own weight, which adds up to 100%. Apple is represented by 6%, Microsoft by 5%, etc. If you invest in an index fund that mirrors the S&P 500, your money will also be distributed based on that weight.

The first index fund was created by **John C Bogle**. He passed away in 2019, but he was the founder of the Vanguard Group. You can still invest in that index fund that he created, and it's still widely popular. It's an index fund that tracks the S&P 500. Now, the first ETF in the US also happens to track the S&P 500, and it's also very popular.

It's called the **SPDR** or also the **SPY**. The S&P 500 is a popular index to use as a benchmark. Also, many money managers and fund managers use it as a benchmark and compare it to the investments that they're managing. They're looking at how the S&P 500 is performing, while trying to outperform the S&P

500. In the short term, they're more than likely able to outperform the S&P 500. The question is, can they do that over the long term?

A major benefit that you have when you invest in index funds or an ETF, is that it eases you into the investing world without you having that much knowledge or experience when it comes to investing. Even for me, the first index fund that I purchased was the **VFINX**, which was the **Vanguard S&P 500 index fund**. That index fund taught me how to gauge the performance of my fund and how emotionally sound I am when I see my money go up but also when I see the value of my investment portfolio go down.

It also taught me about the 500 companies that I'm invested in and what's the specific weight by company. And one thing that I immediately noticed was that tech companies had more weight in that specific portfolio, the S&P 500. Another thing that I noticed was that every quarter I was getting paid a dividend. So I was able to track my dividends and ensure that my dividends would get reinvested back into the fund. So not only am I getting my capital gains, which is my investment increasing in value, but I'm also getting dividend payments.

What I also appreciated was that I was immediately diversified when investing in an index fund. So, in the case of the S&P 500 investing in 500 companies, I don't have to go out there and do the research on which companies I need to add to my portfolio. I didn't have to cherry-pick every single company just investing in the index fund.

And I don't have to manage and maintain those companies because if a company isn't performing well according to the standards of the S&P 500, those get kicked out, and then new ones are introduced into the S&P 500. So, since the index fund mirrors the underlying index it tracks, you will also have those new companies in your portfolio.

Index funds vs ETFs
What's the difference between the two? What should you be paying attention to? Which one should you focus on? When I first started investing, I focused on index funds, but I like ETFs better now.

And there's three reasons why I like the ETFs better. The first one has to do with the fees associated with index funds and ETFs. If you take a bunch of index funds and you compare them to their equivalent ETFs, you'll notice that the fees on the ETFs are slightly lower than the fees of the index funds, especially if you take a mutual fund and you compare the fees or the expense ratio with the equivalent ETF.

You'll be blown away and shocked at how much you're paying in fees for the mutual fund. And like I always say, any money that you can save in fees is money that you can invest in building and growing your wealth.

The second reason is that you can trade with ETFs just like how you can buy and sell stocks. So, you can buy and sell whenever you want throughout the trading day. This is not something that you can do with an index fund, because with an index fund or even a mutual fund, you can only trade at the end of the trading day. But with an ETF, you can trade in the morning, midday, or even before the market closes. That's a big benefit.

And the third reason for choosing an ETF over an index fund is because, with an ETF, you can participate in options trading. This is not something that you can do with an index fund, but a lot of investors like ETFs because of the options trading component attached to the ETF.

The ETF is on face value also cheaper than the index fund. When I invested in the VFINX index fund, I had to put $3,000 down just to get into that S&P 500 index fund.

With the ETF, I can buy a single ETF of that same equivalent, which is currently around $300 and start trading.

4 Best Funds

So, the first one on the list is the **VOO**, which stands for the **Vanguard 500 Index Fund ETF**. This is the ETF, if you want the index fund equivalent, you want to take a look at the **VFINX** or the **VFIAX**. Now, **VOO** is one of my personal favorites. It's also the first ETF that I started investing in. With the **VOO**, you're just trying to match the market. You're not trying to beat the market because with the **VOO,** you're mirroring the companies that are in the S&P 500, which is being used as the benchmark.

The second one is the **BND**. This is the **Total Bond Market Index Fund ETF**. The cool thing about this one is that if you look at the top securities in this fund, they are all **Treasury notes**. And the Treasury note has a maturity date of between two and ten years. All those Treasury notes have different maturity dates, and they have different interest payment dates. So, with a normal Treasury note, you get paid once every six months. But in the bond ETF, you get paid monthly. And even if a bond matures, you don't have to go out and buy new bonds because you can just be invested in BND, hold on to it, and you'll start getting interest payments monthly!

The third one is **VTWO**, which is the **Vanguard Russell 2000 Index Fund ETF**. This ETF mirrors the **Russell 2000**, the Russell 2000 tracks 2000 small-cap companies. The good thing about these small-cap companies is that they have the potential to blow up and become **mid-cap** or even **large-cap** companies.

Also, small-cap companies don't have as many eyeballs as mid and large-cap companies. So, there are a lot of hidden gems that first become available in that Russell 2000.

Number four is the **VXUS**, which is the **Vanguard Total International Stock Index Fund ETF**. If you're the type of investor that wants to invest globally or internationally, you more than likely know that by investing internationally, a whole new set of risks come into play that you normally don't have to think about; economic risks, companies paying out dividends, but not as consistently as companies within the US, shady business practices, etc. There are a lot of risks associated with investing in companies in countries that you might not be familiar with. That's where this ETF plays a big role in your investment portfolio.

And I have an interesting story about international investing. I like to invest in individual companies, but I also like to invest in index funds and ETFs. And I was looking at investing in some companies in different countries. I was looking at investing in companies internationally, so I was looking at different countries and continents, and I was using a stock screener in order to plug in my numbers to see which companies I could add to my watchlist and then eventually buy.

I was looking in Brazil, countries in Africa, China, and India, where I found a handful of good companies to invest in. One of them was in China, which was **China Mobile**. So, I went ahead and paid about $300 to $400 to buy stock in China Mobile. I was collecting the dividends on a frequent basis, and I was watching the value go up and down like it always does in the stock market. However, a couple of months after I bought it, the US government banned China Mobile.

They did give me a heads-up a couple of months before the ban. But I'm the type of investor that doesn't always look at my investment accounts on a frequent basis, especially my international investment account. What ended up happening was that when I actually logged in to my account, I noticed that the ticker symbol for China Mobile was turned into numbers. So I tried to sell it after I knew what had happened and I couldn't sell it for a couple of months because of the ban. And that's where an International Stock ETF Fund would be perfect because a fund manager is always up on the latest information.

So, in this case, the fund manager would take the necessary actions in order to sell China mobile before the ban went into effect.

Number 5 is called **VO** (Vanguard Mid-Cap ETF), which invests in mid-cap companies. VO has between 300 and 400 companies in its index. These are companies that could also turn into large-cap companies.

So, we've hit the large-cap companies with the VOO, and we've hit the small-cap companies with the VTWO, which invests in the Russell 2000 companies.

We've also hit the bond market, which is the fixed income asset, with the BND ETF. But if you also want to round it up, large-cap, small-cap, and then mid-cap, make sure you take a look at VO.

Now you might be thinking why all these ETFs and index funds are Vanguard specific ones. Well, you can look at the equivalent ETFs and index funds from different companies, such as Fidelity, but you will more than likely notice that Vanguard has the lowest expense ratio when it comes to their ETFs and index funds.

Index Fund Research
How do you do the research to make sure that you're investing in the correct index fund or ETF that has a proven track record of success? There are two things that I pay attention to: the management team and the fund's performance.

Whenever you're investing, even in a mutual fund, index fund, or ETF, you always want to pay attention to the track record of the management team. How long have they been managing the fund? How long have they been in the business? The investing world is extremely competitive, so if you don't perform, you're not going to last very long. So, if you can find a mutual fund, an index fund or an ETF that has a track record of success with the management team, it is more than likely that will be a good one to stick with.

For example, I'm going to pick on the VFIAX, the Vanguard 500 Index Fund Admiral Shares. You can go to Morningstar, type in that ticker symbol, and you will get some results. What you want to do is go to the people section. The people section will show you the management team. I already did the research, and I noticed that Donald and Michelle are both on the management team managing this specific index fund. They've both been managing this index fund for over five years. Not only that, but you can also get information on how long they've been in the business and their educational history, which also helps when making the decision to invest.
So looking at these two fund managers, Donald has been managing different funds since 1997, and Michelle has been managing different funds since 2017. And then, of course, the second metric is performance.

You can still research performance on Morningstar, but you can also go to Yahoo! Finance. Just stick with the free option, don't pay for this stuff. Sticking with Morningstar, just scroll over to the performance tab, and you'll see a graph with a benchmark, more than likely the S&P 500, and then the index fund, mutual fund, or ETF that you chose.

Growth of 10,000

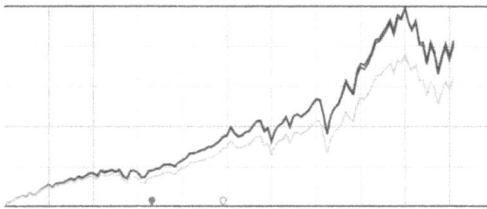

And you can compare the two. You can see how your index fund performed compared to that S&P 500 benchmark. Pretty much what you're looking for is your index fund, your ETF, or your mutual fund needs to beat that benchmark.

Index Funds and ETFs Popularity

Now, where do I see the popularity of ETFs and index funds going into the future? I think they're going to get even more popular, maybe not with the younger crowd, because the younger crowd wants invest in a lot riskier securities like volatile stocks or crypto. They want to make their money fast. They want to become a millionaire fast. But for the older crowd, 30 and up, are more than likely going to focus on ETFs and index funds compared to mutual funds and investing in individual stocks.

Chapter 4: Growth vs Income Stocks

Let's touch on growth versus value investing. Or you could also say growth stocks versus value stocks or even income stocks. Now, with these two different stocks, there are also two different methods to make money. Investors buy growth stocks because growth stocks have the possibility to grow in value faster than what the average stock market will do on a year-to-year basis. So, if the average stock market increases by 8 to 11% in a good year, growth stocks can easily double that. So, you can see a growth stock that might increase by 20, 40, 80, 300% in one year!

A company or a stock such as Tesla can do that. Now, with a value stock, these are companies that are blue chip companies. These are more stable and consistent companies. They might not be the most exciting companies. They might not have products or services that are exciting to investors, but they do have a consistency that a lot of investors like and they also pay out a dividend. These are companies such as Walmart or even Fastenal, which is a company that sells screws and construction equipment. This company is not really that interesting when it comes to the product that they sell, but they do generate revenue and profits on a consistent basis, which they also grow but not as fast as a growth stock would be able to grow its revenue.

So, the primary way of making money with a growth stock versus a value stock, it's the mindset that you have as an investor because if you invest in a growth stock, you only care about the stock price going as high as it can and then potentially selling it and making a profit.

So, your mindset is focused on making a profit through capital gains. With a value stock, you're focusing on the stock giving you a consistent income in the form of a dividend. The value of the stock can also jump up in value, but that's not the primary reason why you buy a value stock. Of course, you can still participate in options trading, and you can still do short selling, but those two are the primary ways of making money with a growth stock versus a value stock.

Growth stocks, in general, don't pay a dividend because any profits that the company makes, they put back into the business to grow the business as fast as possible. A growth stock can be in pretty much any industry or sector, but you will definitely see growth stocks in the technology sector. And if you think about it, with technology, you have to be creative. You must do a lot of research, and you have to beat out the competition. So, instead of taking some of that profit and paying it out as a dividend to the investor, you want to grow the company as fast as possible because, in the tech sector, there's too much competition. So, it's best to take the profit that the company generates and put it back into the business in order to stay competitive.

Some of the things that a company can do with the profits that they put back into the business are research and development, coming up with more creative ways to promote their products, updating their equipment, expanding into different locations, etc. There are various things that the company can do with the income it generates to promote future growth.

Take, for example, a company like Tesla, which sells electric cars and is widely known. If Tesla came out with a new product, an electric car that can drive on land, sea and it can also fly. Just coming out with news like this more than likely will hype up investors to buy more shares in the company, which will potentially make the value of the stock go up even more. This is an example of what profits reinvested into the company can achieve, though it might be a bit of an exaggerated example.

P/E Ratio Explained

And since growth investors like to invest in companies that can increase in value faster than the average stock market performance year over year, these investors don't pay that much attention to the P/E ratio of a company, which is the price-to-earnings ratio.

The price-to-earnings ratio tells you how much price you are willing to pay for the earnings of a company. This is a metric that you pay attention to if you're a value investor. Most value investors will look at P/E ratios of 20 or less. But for a growth investor, since they predict that the sales revenue and earnings of a company will keep growing year over year, the P/E ratio is not something that they primarily pay attention to.

The P/E ratio, is the price divided by the earnings per share. The earnings are the same as the net profit of a company. To calculate the earnings, all you must do is look at the net profit of a company and divide it by the common **shares outstanding**. For example, let's say a company made $2 million in net profit but they have only 1 million shares outstanding. The earnings would be $2 million in net profit, divided by 1 million common shares outstanding, which is $2 in earnings per share.

The price is the stated price that you see on the stock market per share. So if a company is trading at $40 and the earnings is $2, the PE ratio is 40 divided by two is 20.

Analyzing Growth Stocks
What are some of the metrics that you need to look at? If you want to analyze a growth stock, then how can you tell if the stock is one that you want to invest in? There are two specific metrics that you can look at.

The first one is the revenue of a company. It needs to grow year over year. And you can look at the net profit of a company. It's a little bit trickier because there are a lot of growth stocks that have a net loss year over year, but their revenue keeps growing at a high pace.

There are some other metrics that you can look at. You can take a look at the **return on equity** and the **return on invested capital**. But when it comes to growth stocks, just looking at those two, the revenue and the net profit, those are the two main metrics that you need to focus on.

Taking Tesla as an example again, Tesla has been able to grow their revenue by 30% to 50%, if you look over the last 5 to 10 years. Take another growth company like Amazon, and you will notice that Amazon has been able to grow about 25% in the last 5 to 10 years. Think about what the average growth is of the stock market. If you look at the S&P 500, you'll see anywhere between 7 to 11% growth year over year. Both Amazon and Tesla have shown more than double in growth year over year.

With a value stock or an income stock, they might not see double digits in growth because that's not the focus. The focus is on consistency. Value stocks will still grow year over year, but the focus is more on the income that they pay in the form of a dividend to their shareholders.

If you look at a stock market decline or a stock market dip, or even a recession, there's something interesting that you will notice between growth and value investing.

When looking at a growth stock, you need to think about the mindset of the investor. They want to buy a stock that will go up in value fast and continue to go up year over year when everything is going well in the stock market. People are more optimistic, they will tend to pay more for a stock and they will buy more shares in specific companies.

With a stock market decline or crash, people get a lot more pessimistic. If you look at the growth stock, instead of going up in value, it's going to dip down, and it's more than likely going to crash. So, investors react by panicking and end up selling their growth stocks.

Meanwhile, with a value stock, they will also take dip in value, but because most value stocks still pay out a dividend, investors are more than likely to hold on to those investments in value stocks because they still get a payment in the form of a dividend on a quarterly basis despite the dire ecomonic situation.

Technical vs Fundamental Analysis

Let's touch on technical versus fundamental analysis and how that plays a specific part in your investing strategy. **Fundamental analysis** is when you look at the financial metrics of a company, how well the company is performing, you look at sales, revenue, book value, return on invested capital, etc.

Technical analysis deals with the analyzing of stock charts and trying to figure out how that stock is trending on the chart screen. Value investors like to focus on the fundamentals of the company and then buy the company when it's selling at a discount. Meanwhile, growth investors don't necessarily focus on fundamental analysis. Some of them do focus on technical analysis, because they want to buy the company at a cheap price and then be able to sell it at a higher price for a capital gain.

There are also a lot of **day traders** and **swing traders** that like to jump into the stock market and buy growth stocks to profit from small price changes in the price of the stock. You can still day trade with value stocks, but the benefit of doing it with growth stocks is that growth stocks have the potential and possibility to increase or decrease in value a lot faster. That's why growth stocks are usually preferred by day traders and swing traders, or even scalpers.

If you're an investor just starting out and you now know about growth versus value investing, you might be thinking to yourself, "which one would be better for my investment portfolio, a growth stock or a value stock?" I always say why not both? I like to invest in both. I like to invest in value stocks for their consistency in income, but I also like to keep my eye on the growth stocks that could shoot to the moon in a matter of months. You're not limited to either or. You can have both in your portfolio.

Investing Risk

You can also look at how much risk you can endure when you're investing in the stock market. If you're somebody that's more risk averse, value stocks will be more in your lane. They're more stable in a stock market decline. They will also go down in value, but you can still hold on to them and collect the dividend compared to the growth stock. Those are the riskier stocks that you can invest in because you're investing in the potential growth of that company.

But keep in mind that growth stocks are more fun than value stocks. Growth stocks produce products or services that are more enticing to investors, like electric cars, music, technology, etc., compared to value stocks which produce products or services that might be a little bit more on the boring side, but there's nothing wrong with being boring and consistent when it comes to investing.

Chapter 5: 5 Best Growth Stocks

Growth stocks are fun, and they are also addictive. There's nothing more exciting than logging in to your brokerage account in the morning just to see how your growth stocks are performing. And most investors love growth stocks because they're all over the news and social media.

Most growth stocks are going to be in the technology sector, but other sectors can also have growth stocks. However, the tech sector is exciting because it is always on the cutting edge of bringing us new technology for us to buy, talk about and play with.

The tech sector is creative. They're coming out with new products, new technology, and people get hyped up about that stuff. Investors also get excited, and then they want to invest in it. They want to see their capital grow. Growth stocks are also the stocks that investors use to potentially grow their wealth the fastest. Those are the stocks that people talk about when you hear the stories of somebody who bought a stock one day and a couple of days later saw their capital gains shoot by 30, 50%, or even more.

Shopify Inc.

The first growth stock that you need to have on your watch list is Shopify. Shopify is an eCommerce platform that allows you to set up your shop online. All you must do is buy the domain, set up your shop and analytics, make sure that you pick the right theme, upload your products, set up your payment processing, and before you know it, you can start making sales; after you do the marketing and advertising of your products, of course.

It's a very easy platform to use. I've also set up a couple of Shopify stores in the past where I would sell anything from fitness equipment or fitness clothes, to women's handbags. Most of your sales are going to come from mobile devices.

From a growth stock perspective, just looking at the financials, Shopify has been able to grow its revenue year over year in the past five years by 50%. That's great because the stock market, on average, grows in a good year by 10 to 11%. So, seeing a company able to grow 50% on average year over year, that's a growth stock that you need to pay attention to.

Netflix Inc.
Number two is Netflix. Netflix is the most popular streaming service because they're doing a great job of

not only expanding into different countries but it also does a great job of keeping its content as diverse as possible. There's content and even games for any type of viewer. If you like horror movies, documentaries, action movies, crime docs, anime, etc. Netflix has content for pretty much everybody.

This has made Netflix grow from a financial standpoint. When I look at the five-year average and the ten-year average, they've been able to grow by 25%. The main reason why Netflix is the market leader in their space and they're able to not only grow their user base but also retain the users that they have is because they constantly come out with good shows that people want to watch and then talk about on social media. As such, most of the revenue that they generate, they put back into the business by producing content that viewers want to see.

Amazon.com Inc.

Number three is Amazon which is a $1.2 trillion company. During the pandemic, Amazon saw their sales soar, while other retail stores and smaller chains saw either their business go bankrupt or slow down tremendously. It's because of Amazon that companies such as Walmart and Target had to speed up their entrance into the eCommerce world.

Amazon set the standard for fast shipping or, in this case, one-day shipping. Most people that I know love buying their products from Amazon, and Amazon is always on the cutting edge with coming out with new ideas and then implementing them as fast as they can.

Looking at Amazon's financials, they generate all of their revenue from three sectors: North America, International, and AWS. Aws stands for Amazon Web Services. Small and big companies that don't want to have their technology infrastructure in-house have the possibility to outsource it to Amazon.

Tesla Inc.
Number four is Tesla. This is a $700 billion company. If you look at their revenue in the past 5 to 10 years, they've been able to grow their revenue by 33 to 50%!

Tesla, being widely popular, the best-selling car used to be the Model 3. But during my research, I've noticed that the Model Y has been picking up steam and is currently the best-selling Tesla car. Tesla is doing very well with selling their electric cars and then also expanding into different countries. Right now, China is one of the fastest-growing markets for Tesla.

Even when I went on vacation to Europe, I went to the Netherlands to visit family. While I was on the highway, I was paying attention to the cars that I saw and one in five cars that I saw in Amsterdam were Tesla cars.

Tesla has been operating at a net loss for many years. It wasn't until 2020 that they turned their net loss into a net profit. But what you need to remember with these growth companies and these growth stocks is that even when they do make a profit their focus will still be on growth. They focus on getting their revenue as high as possible because they want to beat out the competition.

Their goal in the early phase of the company is to grow, even if that means operating at a net loss for many years. All they then need to do is make a couple of tweaks to turn their net loss into a net profit.

Spotify Technology SA
Number five is Spotify which is not as big as the Amazons or the Tesla's out there, because Spotify is a $16 billion company and it's also operating at a net loss.

But Spotify has been making a lot of headway into also growing as fast as possible because they started making waves in the music industry. Then they got into podcasting, and now they just added audiobooks. So, they have three pillars on which to grow now, the three-headed monster. Spotify wants to dominate the audio space; they want to capture your ear. And Spotify always comes up with new ideas, cutting-edge technology, anything that they can do to make it easier for their listeners to enjoy the platform.

Spotify is also good at monetizing the user base that they have. They have the subscription model, they have ads that are running, but then they also have a retail model, which they introduced when they added audiobooks to their platform.

Why are these the five growth companies to keep an eye on? The reason why you want to take a look at these five companies is because they are not only dominant in their space, they're the leaders in their space. They're also seeing record year-over-year growth, and they're also not going to go away anytime soon.

Most people know about them. Most people talk about them, which makes them even more popular. Your cousin might talk about them, or your uncle might talk about buying them. Also, the mainstream media is talking about these companies. Not only are they popular now, but they're also going to be more than likely popular in the future because these companies are always on the cutting edge when it comes to technology within their space, making sure that they come up with creative ways to retain their customers. The management team is also doing a great job of managing the day-to-day business.

Market Capitalization
Another thing that you need to pay attention to is that all these companies that I mentioned are large to mega-cap stocks. **Market capitalization** shows you the value of a company, in other words, how much a company is worth.

So, when I say a company like Tesla is worth $700 Billion, that goes to the market cap of the company. The market cap is calculated by taking the price of a single share and multiplying it by the outstanding common shares. If a company has a $50 price for their stock and they have 1 million shares outstanding, the market cap is 50 times 1 million is $50 million. Depending on the value of a company, it will fall under a specific cap.

A company that is worth $300 million or less is going to be a micro-cap, anywhere between $300 million to $2 billion, that's going to be a small cap company, $2 billion to $10 billion, that's going to be a mid-cap, $10 billion to $200 billion is going to be a large cap. And anything over $200 billion is going to be a mega-cap company.

I focused on large and mega-cap companies. But you can also take a look at micro-cap, small-cap and even mid-cap companies, because those companies, even though they might not be as famous as the large and mega-cap companies, they still have potential because there are not that many eyes on those types of companies. But they have the potential to blow up also and become large-cap or even mega-cap companies. Of course, a lot of risk is involved in all these companies. It doesn't matter if they're a small-cap company or a large-cap company. Always remember that investing will always bring with it a certain amount of risk.

Stock Market Indexes
If you want to know which indexes these companies are trading on, look no further than the **S&P 500**, which is the Standard and Poor's 500, which contains

the 500 largest companies in the US. Another index is the Nasdaq 100. The NASDAQ 100 is similar to the S&P 500. However, it has fewer stocks in its index, but most of the stocks are highly focused on the technology sector, which is all of the stocks that I mentioned in the top five list. And even if you look at the top six companies in the NASDAQ 100, the top six companies take up 37% of the whole index! Some of those companies are going to be Microsoft, Google, Amazon, Apple, and even Tesla.

Another index that's widely popular is the **Russell 2000**, which is an index of approximately the 2000 biggest small-cap companies. There's a lot of potential in the Russell 2000 if you want to invest in it. All you have to do is find an index that mirrors the Russell 2000. Or you could also do the research and make sure that some of the companies in the Russell 2000 have seen year-over-year growth past the average of what the Russell 2000 does on a yearly basis. Those will be some of the companies that you want to pay attention to. Make sure you look at their business model. Is it one that can grow into the future? Is it one that will need to change? Does it have stability? If that company is a small-cap company right now, does it have the potential to become a mid-cap company or even a large-cap company?

Make sure you also take a look at the management team and how they are performing on a day-to-day basis. These are some of the things that I would pay attention to if I wanted to invest in a small-cap company that's in the Russell 2000. But starting out, I would focus on an index fund that just mirrors the Russell 2000.

Another index is the **Wilshire 5000**. This index contains all the publicly traded companies in the US. If you want to invest in all of the companies in the US, whether it be small-cap, micro-cap, large-cap, mid-cap, or even mega-cap, the Wilshire 5000 would be the one you would need to invest in. It's not necessarily one of my favorites because I like to be a lot more detailed and analyze specific companies that I want to invest in.

But if you just want to have a basket of literally all the companies, the Wilshire 5000 is the one that you need to pay attention to. When the Wilshire 5000 was introduced, it had 5000 companies in the index. Currently, it has about 3300 to 3500 companies, anywhere in between.

And the last one is the penny stock market, the **OTC market**. This is an interesting market because there are a lot of companies that couldn't or would not get on the more reputable stock exchanges, for example, the Nasdaq, because there are rules to get on the stock exchanges. Some of the rules will be that a company that wants to get on a specific stock exchange needs to be able to generate a specific amount of revenue year over year.

A company also needs to be able to keep its stock price above one dollar because if it fall below $1 for a period of time, let's say six months, it will get a notification that they're going to be potentially de-platformed from the stock exchange.

The penny stock market is extremely risky because most of those companies don't even need to register their financials with the SEC. So, a lot of risks are involved in the penny stock market, plus the trading volume is not that liquid. So, it's not as easy to buy and sell stocks compared to some of the more popular stock exchanges. So be careful with the penny stock market! I don't like to dabble in the OTC market, but there are a lot of investors that take a peek and try their hand at the penny stock market.

Initial Public Offering

So, with growth companies, the focus is on growth, as mentioned earlier. Growing the company as fast as possible because they might want to grow into different states, they might grow their business into different countries. They might want to introduce new products and produce them on a mass scale, they might need to hire more employees, even if all this means operating at a net loss.

One of the things that a company can look at, if they are a private company, is to go through the **IPO** process, which is the initial public offering. This is a process where a private company turns into a public company by being listed on the stock market. This is a great way for a company to generate a large amount of capital. When a company goes from being a private company to a public company through the IPO process, that does not guarantee that this company will be profitable.

Also, one of the disadvantages of a private company going public is that all the financials of the company also need to be made public for investors and the public. A private company does not have to publish any report or even show any of its financials. But publicly traded companies need to do that. Another disadvantage is that your competition also has access to all your financial data, and they can use it in whatever way they see fit.

Always remember that when it comes to investing - it doesn't matter if it's a growth stock, a dividend-paying stock, or if you're investing in a penny stock, always know that it's risky. There's always risk involved when it comes to investing.

Chapter 6: How to Invest $500-1000

You're ready to start investing, but you might only have a small amount of money. That's why I want to address how to start investing if you only have $500 to $1000. This is an interesting topic because I'm going to be making a lot of assumptions. If you have $500 to invest, which is a good amount of capital, but it's still a low amount of capital if you look at the long term of your investing journey because eventually, you will want to invest more than $500.

But if you have $500 to $1000, what I want you to take away is the thought process and the mindset. Your situation is more than likely different. So, you might have less than $500 to invest, you might only have $300, or you might have more than $1,000 to invest. You might have $5000 or even $10,000. When I started out, I had between $5,000 to $10,000 of capital to invest.

You can take this information and then apply it to your own situation and start building your own wealth. Some of the topics that I will mention are going to be stocks, ETFs, and bonds. I'm going to skip the index funds because, with the more popular index funds, you're going to have to put down a large amount of capital just to start investing in them. For example, if you take the popular Vanguard S&P 500 index fund, which is the VFINX, the minimum amount is $3000 to start investing in that fund.

So, that's why we will leave the index funds on the side for now and focus on their ETF equivalent. I'm also going to look at aggressive and conservative portfolios.

$500 Investment Portfolios
The first one we will look at is the aggressive $500 portfolio. Now, when I say aggressive, I'm talking about how risky and how risk averse you are when it comes to investing because the riskier investments are going to be stocks, fixed income assets such as bonds are going to bring stability to your portfolio. In a bull market, everything is looking great. Stocks are shooting up, but in the bear market, stocks are dipping down. And your bond, your fixed-income asset, will provide stability to your portfolio.

The first thing that you want to pay attention to when it comes to your $500 aggressive portfolio is the VOO ETF, which is the Vanguard 500 Index Fund ETF. You want to buy one share of this ETF. Currently, it's priced at $366. The next one you want to look at is the VXUS, which currently is only about $52. You only want to buy one share of that ETF as well. The VXUS is the Vanguard Total International Stock Index Fund ETF. And since this is a total international ETF, you're also capturing high-quality companies outside of the US. The last ETF that you want to have in your $500 aggressive portfolio is the BND ETF, which stands for the Vanguard Total Bond Market Index Fund ETF.

Aggressive $500 Portfolio

VOO	$366	75%
VXUS	$52	11%
BND	$72	15%
Total	$490	100%

Vanguard 500 index fund ETF
Vanguard total international stock index fund ETF
Vanguard total bond market index fund ETF

So, we have $366 for VOO and $52 for VXUS, which is the international stock index fund ETF. And then you have $72 for BND. If you break it out by how risky your portfolio is, your fixed income assets, which is the BND, accounts for 15% of your portfolio.

Now, the other 85% consists of stocks, both the S&P 500 stocks and then also international stocks. So, with the S&P 500 ETF and then also the VXUS, which is the total international ETF, you have that immediate

diversification in high-quality companies. And then, with the BND, you have that fixed-income asset that provides stability to your portfolio.

This is a very aggressive portfolio because only 15% of your portfolio is in a stable fixed-income asset. If you add up all these three ETFs, you'll pay about $490. So you still have $10 left to buy a fraction of a share. Or you can also invest it in **crypto**.

If you move over to the conservative $500 portfolio, we're going to make some slight changes. We're going to keep the VOO, that's the foundation of your portfolio, and we're going to buy two BND shares, which will bring your fixed income assets to 28% and your stocks to 72%. If you add this all up, you'll get a little over $500. You'll get to $510. The reason why this is more on the conservative side is that you have 28% of your portfolio in a fixed-income asset.

Conservative $500 portfolio

VOO	$366	72%
BND (2x)	$144	28%
Total	$510	100%

Vanguard 500 index fund ETF
Vanguard total bond market index fund ETF

The way I think about fixed-income assets and **asset allocation** is to use the John Bogle method. This method says that whatever your age is should be your percentage in fixed income assets such as bonds, certificates of deposits, savings accounts, etc.

So when we look at bonds, I'm going to take 30 years as the average. I'm just assuming that we are all 30 years now. Depending on how risk-averse or how risky you want to get with your investing, you don't have to put 30% in bonds. You can go even less or even a little bit more. So, let's say you are 30 years old, but you only want to have 20% in fixed-income assets. Just tailor your portfolio to hit that correct percentage.

$1,000 Investment Portfolios

You have probably already noticed with the conservative portfolio, we got rid of the total international ETF. If we now move over to the aggressive $1,000 portfolio, now it gets a little bit more fun and a little bit more interesting because we're going to introduce some individual stocks.

We're still going to keep the same ETFs, but we're going to add some additional stocks to it. Also, I want you to add two growth stocks and two dividend-paying stocks of your choosing, but make sure you still hit that $1,000. It's fine to go slightly over or slightly under but try to keep it in the $1,000 range. We have VOO, which is the foundation of the portfolio. We have one for VXUS, which is the International Stock ETF, we have two BND, we have one Tesla, which is a growth stock, we have one Amazon stock, also a growth stock, and then we have two dividend-paying stocks.

The first one is Realty Income and the second one is Nike. Looking at the cost: VOO at $366, VXUS at $52, BND since we have two at $144, Tesla at $194 currently, Amazon at $99, Realty Income at $64, and Nike at $105. If you add all these up, you're a little bit over $1,000. You are at $1,024.

These are the two individual dividend-paying stocks and growth stocks that I choose. You can switch them out and pick your favorites with this aggressive $1,000 portfolio.

Also, similar to the aggressive $500 portfolio. With the aggressive one, we have 14% in fixed income assets because we bought the BND ETF.

Aggressive $1,000 Portfolio

VOO	$366	36%
VXUS	$52	5%
BND (2x)	$144	14%
TSLA	$194	19%
AMZN	$99	10%
O	$64	6%
NKE	$105	10%
Total	$1,024	100%

Vanguard 500 index fund ETF
Vanguard total international stock index fund ETF
Vanguard total bond market index fund ETF
Tesla
Amazon
Realty Income
Nike

Moving over to the more conservative $1,000 portfolio, we're going to keep the same stocks and ETFs, but we're going to make some slight changes. What I'm going to do is we're only going to have one growth stock and one dividend-paying stock, and we're going to go up on our fixed income asset because we want to get it into that 30% range, based on our imaginary age of 30 years old.

We're still going to keep VOO, which is $366. For VXUS, we're going to keep one. We're going to up BND from 2 to 4 shares, I'll keep Tesla, and I'm keeping Realty Income. Realty Income is a monthly dividend-paying stock. So, you'll have the benefit of seeing monthly dividend payments from this Real

Estate Investment Trust deposited in your account with this conservative portfolio. Your fixed income assets, your bonds, are at 30%, and then 70% are in stocks with this asset-allocated conservative portfolio.

Conservative $1,000 portfolio

VOO	$366	38%
VXUS	$52	5%
BND (4x)	$288	30%
TSLA	$194	20%
O	$64	7%
Total	$964	100%

Vanguard 500 index fund ETF
Vanguard total international stock index fund ETF
Vanguard total bond market index fund ETF
Tesla
Realty Income

If you add up all your capital, you will spend about $964 in this portfolio. So, you still have a little bit of leg room. You still have a couple of dollars to invest in a different security. With the portfolios that I just talked about, you can take both the aggressive and the conservative and then apply them to your own situation. You might want to fudge some of the numbers a little bit, maybe switch out a stock here or there, and then make it your own. If you have more than $1,000 to invest, you can just adjust the aggressive or conservative portfolio based on your asset allocation.

Opening a Brokerage Account

You might be ready to start investing, but you have no idea where to start. Nowadays, it's extremely easy to start investing because all you need is a brokerage account. Some of the more popular ones are going to be Robinhood, Ally, TD Ameritrade, and E*Trade. You have a plethora of options. All you do is go to the particular brokerage firm's website, fill out your personal information, get your login info, deposit your capital, and you're ready to go.

Make sure that you only invest when you're starting out during business hours. Don't trade during the after hours, either pre-market or after the market closes, because that's another level of risk that, if you're just starting out investing, you don't want to mess with.

Another cool thing about brokerage firms nowadays is that you don't have to pay commission fees when you buy or sell shares. Back when I first started out investing, I had to pay $5.99 to $6.95 just to buy and sell stocks. But nowadays, brokerage firms have different ways to make money, such as order routing, which allows them to give you commission-free trading.

And even if you have less than $500 to invest, you might only have $100 to invest. Still, go ahead and start investing because you can buy **fractional shares,** so you don't even need to worry about buying a whole share. You can buy a fractional share of, let's say, a company such as Apple or even Amazon. If a company pays a dividend, if you buy a fraction of that share, you also get a fraction of that dividend. So even if you only have $50 or $100 and you want to invest in Coke, but you think that you don't have enough money, go ahead and buy the fractional share, and then you also get that fractional dividend.

The next thing you will notice about investing with a low amount of capital is that emotionally, you'll be able to handle the ups and downs of the stock market better because if you only have a small amount of capital invested, you're going to be less inclined to make immediate decisions when it comes to selling stock when you see the value of your stock dip down. Now, what's not going to happen with only $500 to $1000 is that you're not going to become a millionaire overnight. You have to be realistic when it comes to investing a small amount of capital.

There are stories out there where somebody had only $10,000 to invest. They started investing in penny stocks, or they started doing some day trading, and they became millionaires. You have to be skeptical when you hear those stories. Is it possible? Yes. Is it probable? No. It's best to look at investing as a long-term journey. So, you start out with a small amount of capital, which might be $100, $500, or even $1,000. You invest your capital, you learn the process of investing, and then you just add more capital to invest on a frequent basis, also called **dollar cost averaging**. But that's how you want to approach investing. Don't look at it as a get-rich-quick scheme. Look at it as you're building your wealth over the long term.

And when you're starting out with a small amount of capital, you'll be able to go through the ups and downs because it's fine to make mistakes. Everybody makes mistakes, even myself. Every now and then, I might buy a stock that ends up being a dud. But since I'm diversified, I have my capital in multiple securities. Even if I take one hit, overall, I'm still sleeping fine. You might also be thinking, You know what? Forget the stock market. I'll take my $500 to $1000, and I'll invest it in the crypto market."

I'm the type of person to tell you, yes, go ahead and do it, but make sure you take calculated risks. Even myself, I'm also invested in the crypto market. What I would recommend is that you have a separate budget for the crypto market. Make sure you invest in the stock market, but then if you want to, you can also invest in the crypto market.

Just keep in mind that the crypto market is also a lot more speculative than the stock market because even if you look at the stock market when it comes to some of the companies that we invest in, the price of the stock should be based on the earnings of a company and how well the company is performing. But when it comes to the crypto market, there are no underlying metrics that you can analyze to figure out how much a crypto is actually worth. So it's all based on speculation.

If you end up investing your first $500 to $1000. Make sure you give yourself a pat on the back because this is a big deal. You might not look at it like that. You might think that, "Oh, I'm only investing a small amount of capital."

But don't look at it like that because it's a mindset shift. You're doing something totally new; you're starting to invest in the stock market, and you might like it so much that you get addicted to it, in a good way, that you will try to find other ways and other methods of generating some capital in order to invest in the stock market and start to get rich.

Chapter 7: 5 Best Dividend Stocks

Dividend stocks are exciting to me because this is where I shine when it comes to investing. There's nothing more interesting and exciting to me than buying a company that pays dividends when it's selling at a discount and then just holding on to it. And while you're holding on to it, you're making passive income or residual income in the form of a dividend every quarter or every month, depending on which company you buy.

But because you also bought it at a discount, you also have the possibility of seeing some capital gains. So, it's a win-win situation for me. It's also more of a set-it-and-forget-it method. You buy it once. If you do the research, you want to buy good companies, of course, and then you just hold on to it and enjoy the passive income that you generate.

Not only do I look at dividend income as a passive way of making money, it's also a way of making money that grows faster than inflation because a lot of companies don't only pay a dividend. They also grow their dividend. Some companies might also pay a special dividend every now and then. So, it's a very hands-off way of investing. It allows me to sleep well at night. So even if the stock market is trending down, I don't lose any sleep because I'm still holding on to my dividend-paying stocks because they still pay me a dividend that increases faster than inflation.

I reinvest that dividend to get more dividend income, and when I'm holding on to the stock, the price still has the potential to bounce back, and I can see my capital gains rise up. Dividend investing might not be a fast way of making money, but it's a stable and consistent way of not only making money but also building wealth.

I can plot my dividend income, for example, in an Excel spreadsheet and track how much money I'm potentially going to make year after year, depending on how much I invest in dividend-paying companies. This is not something that I can do as efficiently by just looking at capital gains because with capital gains, the stock price or your investments are going to fluctuate year over year. So, you might see that in one year, your investments grow by 9%, but the next year your stocks might have actually lost and dipped down in value.

Nike Inc

The first dividend-paying company is Nike. Now, Nike is famous for their footwear, of course, that's how Phil Knight started the company, by selling shoes. But Nike is known for more than just their shoes. They also sell fitness clothes. And when it comes to endorsements, Nike has partnered with the best athletes in their respective sports. Athletes such as LeBron James, Michael Jordan, Rafael Nadal, Tiger Woods, and the list goes on.

Whenever any of these athletes wear Nike clothing, it brings their fans to Nike, and of course, it brings visibility to Nike. The three main brands that Nike owns are going to be Nike, Jordan, and Converse. From a dividend perspective, Nike has paid a continuous dividend since 1997. That's more than 20 years! They grow their dividend, if you look at the 5 to 10-year average, by 11%. And their **payout ratio** is at 35%.

The payout ratio explained in simple terms; you take the net income that a company generates, and a portion of that net income is paid out as a dividend to the shareholders. For Nike, it's 35%. I like it at 35% because a company that has a higher payout ratio, let's say 90%, If it has a bad year when it comes to their net profit or net loss, it might not be able to pay out a dividend.

So, having that cushion of 65% because they only pay 35% out as a dividend is what I like because they have a cushion where they can still raise the dividend and not be in any financial problems. Also, a fun way of looking at this company is whenever you own Nike shares, if you see somebody walking around outside in Air Jordans shoes or even Nike clothing, a portion of that sale is going to come to you as a dividend because you're a shareholder.

Abbvie Inc

The second company on the list is AbbVie. Now, Abbvie is in the health care sector. It's a biopharmaceutical company. In layman's terms, they create medicine to try to get rid of illness. It's a $255 Billion company, and this is actually a spin-off because in 2013, they spun off Abbott Laboratories. From a dividend perspective, this company has paid an increasing dividend since 2013, and they've been able to grow their dividend by 20%, on average, year over year since 2013. From a payout ratio standpoint, their payout ratio is higher than what we saw with Nike. Their payout ratio is at 74%, but they've been able to consistently generate revenue and they've been able to grow their revenue between 11 to 15%, which also means that they've been able to grow their dividend.

Microsoft Corp

Number three on the list is Microsoft. The funny thing about Microsoft is that most people don't focus on Microsoft compared to other companies. Companies that you always hear about are going to be your Teslas, Google, Facebook, and even Apple. But Microsoft is a $1.6 trillion company. One thing that's interesting about Microsoft is that they have their hands in so many different business ventures, not something that I necessarily like, but it works for Microsoft, they have Windows, GitHub, Xbox, Azure, which is a competitor of AWS, which is a technology infrastructure. Microsoft is doing extremely well. And from a dividend perspective, this company has paid a continuous dividend since 2003.

They've been able to grow their dividend on average by 11% year over year and their payout ratio is at 25%. So everything is pretty much up and up for Microsoft.

PepsiCo, Inc.

Number four on the list is PepsiCo. The Pepsi company is a $244 Billion company. What I like about this company is that it's extremely easy to explain what they do, even to a little kid, because Pepsi produces beverage drinks. But that's not the only thing that Pepsi does. Pepsi owns a slew of brands such as Gatorade, Lay's Potato Chips, Doritos, Quaker Oats, and the list goes on.

From a dividend perspective, Pepsico has paid a continuous dividend since 1973. That's almost 50 continuous years! And not only have they been able to pay a continuous dividend since 1973, they've also been able to grow their dividend. If I look at the last 5 to 10 years, by around 6%. Their payout ratio is a little bit higher at 64%.

But with the track record of Pepsi Company paying out an increasing dividend, they've been through so many economic bumps. Think about the Great Recession, and the Y2K crash. Even through all those dips in the stock market, the Pepsi company has been able to still pay a dividend and increase its dividend above the average inflation rate. That's why I like the Pepsi company, and I have them on my watch list. I also bought stock in the company.

Unilever Plc

And for number five, I want to throw in a different company, a company outside of the US, because number one through four were US companies. This one is outside of the US. It sells famous products, also, and it's the Unilever company.

The Unilever company is a British consumer goods company. So, this is a UK-owned company. You know some of the brands that they own, you've heard of them, but you never thought they were owned by Unilever. These brands are going to be Ben and Jerry's, Dove, Hellmann's, think about the mayo. From an investing standpoint, there's something interesting about companies that are outside of the US.

Now, some of these companies still pay increasing dividends. But you will notice that the dividend amount that is paid out is not consistent because it goes up and down. But if you look at a long-term dividend amount trend. You'll see the trend be an upward trend.

Unilever has paid a consistent dividend since 2008, and they've been able to grow their dividend by around 6%. Their payout ratio, is kept at around 64%.

So, all in all, Unilever is one that you need to have on your watch list and buy when it's trading at a discount.

American Depositary Receipts

ADR stands for American Depositary Receipt. If you want to invest in a company outside of the US, just keep in mind that not all great companies are just within the US. Outside of the US, there are also companies that you might want in your portfolio, for example, Unilever.

If a company wants to go public and be traded on a stock exchange, it usually does that within the country that it's in. So, in the US, for example, we have the Nasdaq and the New York Stock Exchange. If you go overseas, let's say London, you have the London Stock Exchange. If you look at Amsterdam, you have the Euronext Amsterdam Stock Exchange and the list goes on.

Most countries have a stock exchange unless they're small and they don't participate in the buying and selling of securities. Most companies are not going to go through the hassle of being listed on different stock exchanges in all these countries. So, a company in Brazil is probably going to be listed on the Brazilian stock exchange, but they're not going to do the due diligence to also be listed on the American stock exchanges and the London Stock Exchange. An ADR then allows you to buy stock in companies that are not in your current country's stock exchanges. So, in the case of Unilever, the ticker symbol being UL, you can buy Unilever on the New York Stock Exchange.

We went over a lot of good information on these dividend-paying companies, but you still want to make sure that you buy them when they're selling at a discount because, as a value investor, you don't want to buy something when it's too expensive. So, a good way of seeing how expensive or cheap a company is is by looking at the price-to-earnings ratio, the P/E ratio. With dividend-paying companies, I like to see a P/E ratio of 15 or less. You can also stick with 20 or less, however, I prefer 15 or less.

Investing in dividend-paying companies is a steady way of building your wealth over time. It's not a fast method that you can see with growth stocks, but with dividend companies, I can plot my dividend income into the future. I cannot do that with growth stocks because they're a lot more volatile. But with dividend-paying companies, I pay attention to the price of the stock, but I also definitely pay attention to the dividend income that I get. And I make sure that whenever I get the dividend income, I invest it back in companies that can grow their dividend.

I take that dividend income and reinvest it into the company, or I take it and I invest it into different companies that pay a dividend. I also take my new capital and invest it in dividend-paying companies that continue to increase their dividend payments. And then some of these dividend-paying companies also pay a special dividend every now and then. So, it's a snowball effect.

Chapter 8: 4 Best Dividend Index ETF Funds

Let's talk about four awesome dividend ETFs and some index funds. I call dividend ETFs autopilot passive income because all you have to do is invest a little bit of money, and you're collecting dividends on a frequent basis. and the best part is that you don't have to do anything for it. It's extremely passive. Another benefit is that you are immediately diversified into different dividend-paying companies that you're getting your income from.

You don't have to go out there and do the fundamental analysis to make sure that you're picking and choosing the correct dividend stocks to purchase to get that dividend income. Also, the fund managers of these dividend index funds and dividend ETFs are managing this dividend ETF and making sure that they're buying and selling the right dividend stocks for that portfolio. All this is a big benefit.

I'm a value investor, which means that I like to analyze companies, add them to my watch list, and buy them at the right moment. But even I see the benefit of having dividend ETFs because it's not only about buying these companies, it's also about managing them, maintaining them, and making sure that the companies that you bought are still good enough to be in your investment portfolio.

And if you're the type of investor that does not have a lot of knowledge or time to analyze individual stocks, a dividend ETF or index fund is the right way to go. Now, can you get rich off dividend ETFs? You definitely can. It's more of a slow process because, with the dividend ETF, the price of your ETF is going to fluctuate but your dividend income, you will get that on a frequent basis. It's more of a slow and steady way of building your wealth, but it's more stable, and it's more consistent. It's something that you can rely on.

If you're just starting out investing and you're really interested in how dividends work, then that's the best place to start. Start out with a dividend ETF, see what type of companies are in your dividend ETF, and then you can take it from there. If you want to take the next step and then invest in individual companies, you have a good baseline to start with just by looking at some of the companies that you are invested in in the dividend ETF.

For this hands-off approach, you will have to pay a fee which is called the expense ratio, but the expense ratio is so low it's worth it. It's worth it to just invest in a dividend ETF compared to using your free time to start analyzing companies.

If you're just starting out, you're not even sure, and you're not even confident in what you're investing in. At least with a dividend ETF, yes, you're paying the expense ratio fee, but you know that you're investing in the right type of fund.

Vanguard Dividend Appreciation ETF

Looking at the first ETF, this one is going to be the **VIG**, which is the Vanguard Dividend Appreciation ETF. If you're looking for the index fund equivalent, you want to go with the **VDADX**, which is the Vanguard Dividend Appreciation Index fund, Admiral shares. Now with this ETF, 97 to 98% of it is invested in US equity, which means US companies, all large-cap companies. Out of those large-cap companies, 20% of those are invested in the financial sector, and the top three companies are UnitedHealth Group, Johnson and Johnson, and Microsoft. This fund has an average 2% when it comes to the dividend yield.

Dividend yield, explained in simple terms means, how much dividend are you getting for the price that you're paying? So, if you paid $100 for an ETF and the dividend yield is 2%, you'll get $2 in dividend income.

The expense ratio is extremely low for the dividend ETF at 0.06%. And going back to the dividend yield, don't look at a lower dividend yield of, let's say, 2% as a bad thing because with that dividend yield of 2%, whenever you get your dividend, you're actually reinvesting that dividend to buy more dividend paying companies, in this case by reinvesting the dividend back in the fund. So, in this case, that 2% allows you to compound your money.

Schwap US dividend equity ETF
Number two is the Schwap US dividend equity ETF also found under the ticker symbol **SCHD**. Now with this particular ETF, 99% of the capital is invested in US equity. All large-cap companies, with the highest percentage being in the financial sector, which is 21%. And then the top three companies are Merck and Company, Amgen, and IBM. This ETF also has a very low expense ratio of 0.06%, and then the dividend yield is a little bit higher at 3%. So, SCHD is a must-have in your investment portfolio.

Vanguard High Dividend Yield ETF
Number three is the Vanguard High Dividend Yield ETF, which you can find under the ticker symbol for **VYM**. And then, if you're looking for the index fund equivalent, that's going to be **VHYAX**, which is the

Vanguard High Yield Dividend Index Fund Admiral. Now with this ETF, 97% to 98% are invested in US equity, also large-cap companies. But the top three sectors, in this case, are going to be financials, consumer staples, and health care. And then the top three companies in this ETF are ExxonMobil, Johnson and Johnson, and J.P. Morgan. This ETF also has a very low expense ratio of 0.06%. And then the dividend yield on this one is also 3%.

Vanguard Real Estate ETF

And number four, is the highest dividend-yielding one, which is the **VNQ**, which is Vanguard Real Estate ETF. Now, in the real estate sector, you will always have a higher dividend because REITs pay a higher amount of their profits out as a dividend. With this particular ETF, 99% to 100% are invested in US equity, mostly mid-cap companies. And then this ETF does have a little bit of a higher expense ratio at 0.12%, but not that high compared to what you will see when you look at mutual funds.

This ETF is 100%, of course, invested in the real estate sector. And then the top three companies are Prologis, American Tower, and Crown Castle Company.

Another great benefit that you have with investing in dividend ETFs compared to a growth ETF is what's happening in the stock market. Because if you think about the bull and bear market, a bull market is whenever the stock market, on average, is trending up, we're in a bull market, but a bear market is the opposite. So whenever the stock market is trending down, we're in a bear market. Whenever the economy is in an uptrend, people are more optimistic, and they spend more money on consumer goods and services. They also spend more money on buying investments. So the stock market is going to rise.

But in a bear market, people are pessimistic. The economy might not be doing too well. We see sky-high inflation, so people might panic and sell their stock, they might sell their shares, and they might even sell their ETFs. So, by investing in a dividend ETF, those can weather the storm better compared to other types of ETFs such as growth stock ETFs.

Dollar Cost Averaging
The easiest way of looking at dividend ETF investing is by also thinking about dollar cost averaging. With dollar cost averaging, you're investing a specific amount of money on a frequent basis. For example, you might be investing $100 every week, or you might

be investing $1,000 every month. With dollar cost averaging, you're allowing yourself to buy stocks, or in this case, ETFs or index funds. It doesn't matter if the price of the ETF is up or down. It always averages out because you're adding more money to your ETF when the stock market is in a bull market, but also when it's in a bear market. That means you're averaging it out. It's a way of investing without being emotional about investing.

You're taking your emotions out of investing because, more than likely, if the stock market is crashing or we are in a downturn or an economic recession, you're less likely to invest. But with dollar cost averaging, you're allowing yourself to invest when stocks and even dividend ETFs or dividend index funds are selling at a discount. So, you're buy them when they're cheap.

Dogs of the Dow

Looking at these dividend ETFs and even thinking about dividend-paying companies, if you want to find good individual stocks, there are a few different methods that you can use. One of those methods is the Dogs of the Dow method at buying dividend-paying companies. With this method, if you look at the Dow Jones Industrial Average, which consists of 30 high-quality blue-chip companies. A blue-chip company is a stable company that is a leader in the market. It has a track record of success, and it's a large-cap company or even a mega-cap company.

The Dow consists of 30 high-quality dividend-paying companies. What you do with this method is you take ten companies out of the 30 that have the highest dividend yield, and you buy them at the beginning of the year. You wait a whole year, and then you apply the same method. Now, the reason why you want to take the ten highest yielding dividend paying companies is because the index of the Dow already has 30 high-quality companies. And if a company has a high dividend yield, that means that the share price is low compared to the dividend yield, which means that in the future, potentially, the price of the stock is going to go up anyway. So, you're having a double effect of collecting the dividend but also waiting for the share price to potentially go up.

Dividend Lists
Another method that a lot of dividend investors like to use is to look at a specific list, such as the Dividend Kings, the Dividend Aristocrats, the Dividend Champions, or the Dividend Achievers. These are lists of dividend-paying companies that have paid a

continuous dividend in the last 10, 25, or even 50 years. So, the Dividend Kings is a list of companies that have paid a continuous dividend for 50-plus years. The Dividend Achievers is a list of companies that have paid a dividend for at least ten years.

One thing to pay attention to, though, even if you look at these lists with companies that have paid a continuous dividend, you want to make sure that on a yearly basis, the dividend growth has been higher than inflation. So, to me, it doesn't matter if a company has been paying out a dividend for 25 years. If they don't increase their dividend on a yearly basis faster than inflation, then that's not a company that I want to invest in!

Dividend ETF vs Dividend Stocks

So why go for an ETF versus an individual stock? Now you can still do both. You don't have to pick and choose one or the other. But with the ETF, like I already mentioned, you have immediate diversification. You have a fund manager or multiple fund managers that are managing that ETF compared to an individual stock where you have to go out, do the research and do the buying and selling. You don't have that immediate diversification because it's just one company.

But what I've noticed by investing in individual companies is that my **dividend yield** is better compared to the dividend ETFs. So if you look at the two, you just have to weigh the risks with the benefits.

Now, another question that you might be thinking of is comparing a dividend ETF versus a growth stock ETF versus an S&P 500 index fund or ETF. Which one of these three should you be paying attention to? Like I always say, you don't have to pick and choose a specific one because the better portfolio would have a specific amount of money invested in each of them. If you want to make it more technical, yes, you can have those three ETFs, dividend, growth, and S&P 500. But then I'm also going to add a bond fund. So, a Bond ETF and an international ETF. And then you can also add some individual companies, whether they might be growth companies or dividend-paying companies into your investment portfolio.

I like dividend ETFs. I'm always going to be a value investor who likes to invest in individual companies, but I see the benefit of investing in ETFs because even myself, I don't always want to analyze specific companies and then always have to manage them, making sure that they pay their dividends on time, make sure that they didn't cut or stop paying a dividend. In an index fund or an index ETF you don't have to worry about all that management because the fund manager is being paid to manage and handle all these different issues that might pop up.

For example, I invested in the Disney Corporation and a couple of other companies when they paid out a dividend, but the Disney Corporation and these other companies ended up stopping their dividend payments shortly after I invested. I was lucky enough to catch most of them at the time that they stopped their dividend payments. But some of them I didn't know about until I logged in to see if I got my dividend payment, and when I noticed that I hadn't, I then had to figure out why.

With a dividend ETF, I wouldn't have to manage all this. I wouldn't have to keep up to date with all these dividend-paying companies. That's why the dividend ETFs and the dividend index funds that I mentioned are a big plus and advantage in my book.

Chapter 9: 401k vs Roth IRA vs Traditional Brokerage Account

I've noticed that there's a lot of confusion when it comes to the different investment accounts that you have access to and then also the different retirement accounts for your retirement. I'm particularly talking about accounts such as the 401k, the IRA, the Roth versions of those accounts, the traditional brokerage account, and then also the self-employment retirement accounts.

A 401k is an employer-sponsored retirement account. Not all employers offer a 401k, but most of them tend to. Previously, employers offered pension plans to their employees, but they all started opting for the 401k instead. With a pension plan, managing your investments was being done for you, but with a 401k, management of this retirement account is being pushed to the employee to control all their investments. With a 401k, you have some options in different securities that you can invest in, such as mutual funds, index funds, ETFs, and even **target date funds**.

The interesting thing about target date funds is that you have an investment that automatically rebalances itself the closer it gets to your retirement age. So, if you have a target date fund that is named "target date fund 2050", that means that the closer we get to the year 2050, the target date fund is automatically going to rebalance itself into a more stable, more conservative investment fund.

Some additional cool things about a 401k is that most companies match your 401k contribution. So, you might see that the company is going to match 4% dollar for dollar. For example, if you make $50,000 as your base salary and you invest 4% of your salary into your 401k, 4% of $50k is $2,000. If a company matches dollar for dollar up to 4%, they'll also add an additional $2,000 to your 401k. So, if you invested the first $2,000, they add a second $2,000. Now you have invested $4k in your retirement account.

Now, you might also see companies that match up to 4%, but they only do $0.50 on the dollar. So, you invest a dollar, and they add $0.50 up to 4%. So, with that same example, if you make $50k and you invest 4%, which is $2k, the company will match $0.50 on your dollar. So, they will match an additional $1,000. Be sure to check if your company matches at the business you work at.

Even though the company matches your contribution, there's still a **vesting period** that you have to look at because even if the company matches you dollar for dollar or dollar to $0.50, if you look at the fine print, you will see that you need to work at a company for a few years before you're 100% vested. It might be four years; it might be five years. Every company is a little bit different. The vesting period shows you how many years you must work at a company before the company match is 100% yours to keep.

You will be limited when it comes to the different options you have to invest in with a 401k. These are always going to be limited by what the company has chosen for it's employees. So, you're going to have a limited amount of index funds to invest in, stocks, ETFs, or target date funds. Being limited by the number of options you have to invest in in the 401k could be a good thing, but it could also be bad.

For an investor like me, that's actually a bad thing because I want to be able to invest in whatever I want to invest in because I do research and analyze companies. But if you're somebody that's new to investing or you're not that well versed when it comes to the stock market, then having a smaller list of options is probably best for you because otherwise, you're going to get confused when you have way too many options to choose from. Some employers also offer you a discount if you buy the company's shares.

There is a limit to how much you can invest into your 401k. Currently, it's a little over $22,000. Every single year it rises a little bit, and if you're older, you can invest some additional contribution to catch up. Currently, it's over $7,000.

Some confusion happens when people talk about a traditional 401k versus a Roth 401k. Everything is the same between the two, with the options you have when it comes to choosing your investments. But you are taxed differently when it comes to the traditional 401k and then the Roth 401k. The easiest way to remember this is that with a Roth 401k, you're investing with after-tax dollars, and with a traditional 401k, you're investing with pretax dollars. With a traditional 401k, when you hit retirement age, and you start taking money out of your retirement account, that's when you're going to get taxed. However, with a Roth IRA, you're already taxed on the money that you've made, and then the money that's left that's the money that you invest in your Roth IRA. When you then hit retirement age, the money that you take out of your retirement account is not taxed at that moment. Now, this could all be subject to change if the government sees fit.

So which option should you go with? The traditional 401k or the Roth 401k? The cool thing about this is that you can have both. So, you're not limited by having only one or the other. You can have both the traditional 401k and Roth 401k. But one thing to think about is if you hit that retirement age, are you planning on being in a higher tax bracket? Because keep in mind with a traditional 401k, you get taxed when you take out your money during retirement age. So, if you think that you'll be in a higher tax bracket, you might want to opt-in for the Roth 401k instead. So, it comes down to whatever works best for your situation at your retirement age.

Even if you have both, they cannot exceed the yearly contribution limit. So, if the limit is $22,500, both your traditional and Roth 401k can only add up to that amount, not taking into account the catch-up contribution.

The money that you invest in your 401k, can you take it out before retirement age? The retirement age is 59 and a half. You want to be careful with taking money out of your 401k because you might get hit with a penalty. If you take money out of your 401k before retirement age, you will have to pay taxes, more than likely. And then you will also get hit with a 10% penalty. There are some situations where you can take some money out of your retirement account. For example, if you're buying your first home or if it's a medical emergency that you need to pay for, there are some exceptions where you can take money out and not be hit with a penalty, but definitely double-check the most recent rules when you want to take any type of money out of your retirement account. You can also borrow some money from your 401k, but you will have to pay it back into your own 401k.

Individual Retirement Account
The IRA is an individual retirement account. You got the traditional IRA, but then you also have the Roth IRA. Like I mentioned previously, If you look at the 401k, you are limited in what you can invest in based on options that have been chosen for you. But with the IRA and the Roth IRA, you have the whole investing world available to you. So, if you open up an IRA account, you can automatically invest in all the stocks, bonds, ETF, mutual funds, index funds, and everything that's out there. That's a great benefit that the IRA has that the 401k does not have. A major limitation of the IRA compared to the 401k, is that the

amount that you can invest in your IRA per year is a lot lower than the 401k. Currently, it's slightly over $6,000. Even with the IRA and the 401k, you're not limited by having either or. So, you can have different 401k accounts in your name. Then you can also have different IRAs, such as the Roth IRA and then the traditional IRA in your name.

The thing that you need to keep in mind is that, yes, you can have a Roth IRA and even a traditional IRA, but both still need to add up to your yearly limit in how much you can invest into your IRAs. A good investor will have multiple accounts because you might max out your 401k and you might have some additional money to invest. So go ahead and open up an IRA and invest that money in your IRA, which also gives you total access to the stock market.

Now, the traditional IRA versus the Roth IRA. With a traditional IRA, you invest with pretax money, and then with the Roth IRA, you invest with after-tax dollars. So, you will not get taxed when you take money out during retirement. And then, with the traditional IRA, you will get taxed at your tax bracket when you take money out during retirement age.

And then, of course, some of the same penalties that you see with the 401k, also apply to your Roth IRA and your traditional IRA. So you're not supposed to take out money before retirement because you'll get hit with the penalty, and you might have to pay some additional taxes. Also, keep in mind that the IRA accounts are not employer-sponsored accounts, so you're not going to get an employer match with these accounts.

If you want to open up an IRA or a Roth IRA account, you will have to do that outside of work. You'll have to go to one of the big-name brokers such as Fidelity, E*Trade, Ally, TD Ameritrade, etc. One thing you need to be careful with is having way too many investment accounts and retirement accounts open.

So, you might work at one company, and you open up a 401k. You then end up moving to a different company. After a year, you open up a new 401k, and then you move to a third company, and you now have a third 401k, and in the meantime, you also opened up a couple of IRA accounts here and there.

What you need to start doing is condensing them and making sure that you don't have too many 401k's out there because it's going to get confusing during tax time, and it's also going to be hard to keep up with having so many different retirement accounts open. If you leave a 401k account open at a previous employer, more than likely, you're going to have to pay some additional management fees, and that's going to come out of your investment.

So, the best thing to do is to roll over your 401k either into the new employer's 401k, or you can also roll over your 401k into your IRA, making sure it matches. So, you want your traditional 401k to roll over into another traditional 401k at your new employer or a traditional IRA. Now whatever you roll it into, make sure that it works for you, because you can take your 401k and roll it over into the new company's 401k, but then you will also be limited by what the company offers.

Or you can take that 401k and then roll it over into an IRA, which pretty much means you will be able to bypass that contribution limit for the IRA, and then you'll be able to invest in whatever you want to invest in.

Traditional Brokerage Account
All this might still be a little bit confusing because you're just starting your investing journey. You have

some amount of money, and you just want to start investing. You don't want to know about penalties. You don't want to know about different rules. You don't want to know about rollovers. What should you do?

Well, the easiest thing you can do is open a **traditional brokerage account**, also just called a brokerage account, with a company like Robinhood Ally, TD Ameritrade, etc. Just open up a brokerage account, and you don't have to worry about penalties, selling your stock, and then getting hit with a fee.

Also, with a traditional brokerage account, you can open up a **margin account**. With a margin account, you're allowed to invest with borrowed money. Investing is already very risky, but then tacking on borrowed money means that you're bringing your investing risk to a new level by investing with a margin account and investing with borrowed money. If your funds don't fall below a certain level, you will not get a margin call. Whenever you get a margin call, this pretty much means that you need to get your funds back up to a specific level by either selling the investments that you own in your margin account or you need to deposit some new capital into your margin account. Investing with a margin account should only be left for the professional investors out there. Don't start opening margin accounts if you're new to investing.

Even if I think about all these different accounts, the way I would do it is if you have an employer-sponsored 401k and they offer a specific match, I would definitely start there. So, make sure you are invested in your 401k, and you're getting the employer match.

The next thing I would do is open up an IRA and invest some additional money into my IRA or Roth IRA, which will give me the option to invest in whatever security I want to invest in. I'm not limited to investing in only specific securities like with the 401k, and then once I have that setup, I would open up a traditional brokerage account and I would use that traditional brokerage account to experiment and have fun with investing.

For example, you can open a Robinhood account, deposit some money in there, start buying shares, fractional shares, dividend-paying stocks, and see how you're able to fare in the stock market and grow your wealth.

If you're self-employed, you also have access to similar retirement accounts. Some of these are going to be the solo 401k, the SEP, which is the simplified employee pension, the simple IRA, and then the defined benefit plan.

Chapter 10: How I Pick My Stocks

I look at specific metrics when I'm deciding to purchase a company or even purchase stock or shares in a company. When I look at my dividend portfolio, I have 23 dividend-paying stocks in it. The metrics that I look at work for both dividend-paying stocks and growth stocks, but one thing that I always pay attention to is even though I'm buying individual companies. I make sure that I'm well diversified into different sectors.

With the stocks in my dividend portfolio, I received 107 dividend payments, that's close to 9 payments per month. I have more shares in specific dividend-paying companies because these companies spit out dividends more frequently that I can use to purchase other dividend-paying companies, which is pretty much a snowball effect of me receiving dividends and then reinvesting those dividends into other dividend-paying companies.

The act of analyzing a company's performance and metrics to decide if you want to add it to your investment portfolio is called fundamental analysis. Fundamental analysis can be done at a high level or in more detail. When I talk about detail, I'm talking about you opening up annual reports, a couple of them, and then analyzing the numbers and trying to figure out how the company is performing. I like to keep it at a high level by looking at specific metrics. Those high-level metrics, I call that the company's report card.

Let's say you have two kids, a son and a daughter. Both bring their report card to you. You look at your son's report card. He has all A's and B's. And then you look at your daughter's report card. She has a couple of A's, a couple of D's, and a few F's.

Now, that's quite concerning because if you look at your son's report card for math, history, and biology, he has all A's. But then, when you look at your daughter's report card, she has an F for biology, and she has a D- for math. So, now you have to do some additional investigation to try to figure out why she has these bad grades.

That's exactly how I look at analyzing companies. I use my high-level metrics to quickly analyze the company to see if the company is doing well or not. And then, if a company is not doing too well, that's when I dive deeper into the metrics to try to figure out what's going on with the company. Is it something that's happening industry-wide or is it something that's specifically happening to that company?

What does the company do?

The first thing that I look at, even before I look at any of the performance metrics when it comes to a company that I want to invest in, is that I try to figure out what the company does. If I know what the company does and I'm able to explain it to somebody, that's already a great step because I don't like to invest in companies that I have no clue what their business model is or their business practices. If you can explain what a company does to a little kid, not only can you explain it to them, but it's also something that you can explain to yourself, and it's a clear sign that you understand at a high level how the company operates.

You want to make sure that you're investing your hard-earned money into a company that you can trust and one that is a reliable and stable. For example, if I take a company like Chipotle, it's easy to explain to even a kid what Chipotle does because all you have to do is drive up to a Chipotle, bring your kid in, and you show them that they sell tacos, burritos, burrito bowls, and even taco salads to customers. That's how the company makes money.

If you take a company like Pepsi or Coca-Cola, that's an easy business model to explain, also, because Pepsi produces beverages. They produce more than beverages, but they are known for their beverage drinks and they sell them through different distribution channels. So you take your kid to a Walmart or to any local grocery store, and you can show them how Pepsi is using Walmart as one of the distribution channels that they sell their products through. One thing you can also do is open a company's annual report and go to the business section, which explains what the company does.

Competitive Advantage

The next thing that I look at is whether a company has a sustainable, long-term competitive advantage. Warren Buffett also calls this a moat. A company that has a competitive advantage over its competitor has a product or service that it can sell and then also increase the price on, and it will not lose any market share. For example, let's say you want to go to a fast-food place and you want a burger. If you want a Big Mac, there's only one place that you can go to get a Big Mac, which is McDonald's. Or if you want a Whopper, there's only one place that you can go to which is going to be Burger King if you want to get a triple Whopper.

Another example, if you grew up using a specific product your whole life, you're more than likely going to favor using that product, especially if your parents or your grandparents used that product. Think about a product such as Colgate or Clorox. If you grew up with these products, it is more than likely you will continue using these products because that's a competitive advantage that this product has. Some companies have what I call **cash cows**. These are products that a company produces, and they never have to change anything about the product over the years. So they can sell the exact same product for years and decades without even changing the product. They still have a loyal fan base. Think about a product like Coca-Cola or Pepsi.

The opposite of a competitive advantage is a product that's a commodity. Think about sugar, chicken, or cement, because there's no competitive advantage with these products. Usually, what companies try to do is lower the price and then get into a price war with the competition. Whenever a company has to lower its price just to stay competitive with the competition, that's not a good business model to grow your sales and your income. Meanwhile, a company that has a competitive advantage can increase the price of its products, and its loyal customers will still go ahead and buy their products.

Revenue & Net Income

Digging into the actual numbers, one thing that I always pay attention to is consistency. So, I'm not going to look at last year's performance. I want to see 5 to 10 years of performance and how the company is trending. So the first thing that I take a look at when I look at the numbers is the total revenue a company generates and the net income. What I'm looking for is a consistent uptrend with the revenue growing 3 to 5% each year. If you look at the graph of a company's total revenue, it's not going to be a straight line upwards.

It's going to go up, and it's going to go down. It might dip down a lot more, but the trend should be an upward trend. And then, when I look at the net income, I'm also making sure that the net income is also increasing, just like how the total revenue is increasing. If a company is able to increase its total revenue but they're not able to increase their net income, that means that the management team is not doing a good job of managing the company and making sure that they're not overspending in certain areas of the business. If a company's revenue is not able to grow. But you do see a company's net income growing. That means that the company is trying everything to cut costs, which is also not a good thing.

A company is able to increase its revenue by selling more products or services, being able to expand into new markets, introducing new products to its customer base, and then also when they raise the price of its products. That's why it's important for a company to have a competitive advantage.

Profit Margin

A quick way that I can tell how well management is performing in a company that I want to purchase is by looking at the profit margin. The profit margin is when you take the net income, and you divide it by the total revenue.

What I'm looking for is consistency over the years. I would like to see my profit margins be in the double digits. So, 10% or more year over year, if the profit margin grows higher than 10%, it is even better. The profit margin pretty much tells me how well management is performing on a day-to-day basis to keep the costs down but keep their sales and revenue high.

Return on Equity

The next metric that I look at is the return on equity metric. This metric shows me how well a company is able to produce income based on its shareholder's equity, which is the capital that shareholders have invested in the company. To calculate the return on equity, let's look at an example. Let's say you have $20,000 to invest, and you invest $10,000 in company A and the remaining $10,000 into company B. In other words, your shareholder's equity in Company A and B is both $10,000.

Now, after about a year, Company A generates $1,000 of net income based on the $10,000 of equity that you put into the company. Company B is able to generate $3,000 based on the $10,000 that you invested in the company. The return on equity for Company A is 10%, $1,000 divided by $10,000. The return on equity for Company B is 30%, $3,000 divided by $10,000. Now, both companies have decided to pay out 50% of their net income as a dividend. So, company A takes that $1,000 and pays out 50%, which is $500, and company B, 50% of the $3,000, is $1,500. The remaining earnings are put back into the company, also called **retained earnings**.

Just looking at this example, you can already see that with the $10,000 that you invested in both companies, you're more than likely going to invest more money into company B because company B is able to generate more income based on your equity.

Return on Invested Capital
Besides the return on equity, another metric that I look at is the return on invested capital because some companies manipulate their return on equity metrics. With the return on invested capital, you take the net income minus the dividends divided by the total capital.

Debt
The next metric that I look at is how much debt a company has because the way a company handles debt is going to be a little bit different than the way you and I handle debt because companies usually use debt in order to expand or manage their business.

When it comes to the debt metric, I like to use the debt-to-equity ratio. The debt-to-equity ratio shows me how much total liabilities a company has compared to the shareholder's equity. I like to see this number below one, but every industry is going to be a little bit different.

Another quick calculation that I like to do is to take the company's total liabilities and then divide it by the income that the company generates before taxes. Pretty much what I'm doing here is, I'm trying to figure out how fast a company can pay off its total liabilities, its debt, with the current income that it generates. What I'm looking for is five years or less. So, if anything bad happened with the economy, how many years would it take for this company to pay down its debt with the income it generates.

Share Buyback

The following metric that I look at is if the company is buying back its shares. The reason why this is important is if a company buys back its shares, it increases your ownership of the company, you don't have to pay taxes on it, and it also increases the earnings.

Let's look at an example. If a company only has ten shares on the market and you own one of those shares. You own 10% of the company, one divided by ten. The company ends up deciding to buy back five of those shares and retire them. Now there are only five shares left. You still own one share of the company, but now your 10% ownership just increased to 20%, one divided by five. And here's the interesting thing, even though your ownership went from 10 to 20%, you did not have to do anything for it.

You also didn't have to pay any taxes on your increase in ownership. However, if you sold your shares or even if you got dividends, then you will have to potentially pay taxes. And then also the third benefit is that if a company buys back its shares, that also means that the earnings per share more than likely is going to increase. If a company generates a million in net income and has a million shares outstanding, the earnings per share is one dollar, 1 million in net income divided by 1 million shares outstanding, that's $1.

But if the company decides to buy back 500,000 shares and retire them. There are now only 500,000 shares outstanding, then the earnings per share just increase to $2 because now you have a million in net income divided by 500,000 shares is $2 in earnings per share.

Any company that can increase its earnings per share is more than likely also going to see an increase in the price of the stock itself because a company that's able to increase its earnings is also a company that's worth more.

Those are the main metrics that I look at, and this works well for growth stocks and dividend-paying stocks. But when it comes to dividend-paying stocks, there are some additional metrics that I look at.

Dividend Growth Rate
The first metric is the dividend growth rate. With this metric, I'm just calculating the growth rate of the dividend year over year. So, if the company paid out $1 in dividends last year and $1.10 this year, then the dividend grew by 10%.

What I'm looking for is a company that can increase its dividend year over year, but they need to be able to increase it faster than inflation. So if inflation on average is 3%, I'd like to see a company that's able to increase its dividend year over year by at least 4%. And there are many blue chip companies that can do this.

One thing that I always do is look at at least ten years of dividend increases and, even better, if there was any economic downturn. I pay attention to those years and what the company has done when it comes to their dividend payment because some companies end up decreasing their dividend payments or even stopping their dividend payments in an economic downturn, for example, companies like GE or even Disney.

That's why I'm always making sure that I'm looking at a longer period of ten-plus years to see if this company was able to pay an increasing dividend faster than inflation.

Dividend Yield

The next dividend metric that I look at is the dividend yield. The dividend yield tells you how much dividend you are getting based on how much you paid for the stock. So you're taking the dividend divided by the stock price. Let's say a stock is priced at $10 on the stock market, and the dividend that they pay out for the whole year is $1. Then your dividend yield is 10%. Most people would want to see high dividend yields, but you always have to be careful because something that you might notice is that companies that have a high dividend yield usually have a lower dividend growth rate, and then some companies that have a low dividend yield usually have a high dividend growth rate. Which one should you choose? It depends.

If a company has a high dividend yield, what that tells you is that up front, you're going to get more dividends for what you pay to get the stock. But the dividend growth might not be that fast. It might not grow faster than inflation. Also, you have to be careful with stocks that have a high dividend yield past 5% because it could mean that the price of the stock is down.

Think about it, if the price comes down, the dividend yield goes up. Usually, if the price of a stock comes down, that means that you need to do some additional investigation to see why the price of the stock is down. It could be something that happened with the company. It could be industry-wide, or it could be caused by an economic change. That's something that you need to investigate further. Another good tip is that you can look at the dividend yield historically to decide if this is just a blip in the road or if this is a concern that you need to pay attention to.

Payout Ratio

The last dividend metric that I want to look at is the payout ratio, which tells you how much dividend a company is paying out of the earnings per share, also called the net income. So what I'm usually looking for is a payout ratio of 40% or less. Every industry is going to be a little bit different.

If a company has a 70% payout ratio and they generate $2 in earnings per share, they will pay out a dollar and 40 cents in dividend income. There is a problem with companies that have a consistently high payout ratio because keep in mind the dividend comes out of the net income. If a company's payout ratio is too high then it might be be the case that when there is an economic downturn and their net income takes a dip, more than likely, the dividend is also going to get reduced or even canceled. Some companies also end up deciding to pay a dividend by taking on debt just to keep their shareholders happy and keep the dividend going. That's not a situation that I like to see for any company.

Now, why do I go through the hassle of analyzing companies, and making sure that they hit their report card metrics, and then adding them to a watch list? The reason why I do it is because it's fun for me. I like to create my passive income using various methods, and one of those methods is to create a consistent dividend income. It's something that I like to do by analyzing these companies, and once I buy these companies, I just have to hold on to them and then reap the benefits of all my work by looking at the dividend income that I get as time goes by.

Chapter 11: Dividend/Growth Investment Portfolio Revealed

My dividend portfolio is something that I set up a few years ago, and even though it's a dividend portfolio, which only contains dividend-paying stocks, I'm also going to add some growth stocks to it in the near future.

Now, the reason why I set this up was that I wanted to try something new back in the day. And when I learned about dividend-paying stocks, it sparked my interest. So, I created a separate account because I already had the 401k and some Roth IRAs. But with my brokerage account that I'm using currently, I set up my dividend portfolio, and now it's a portfolio that manages itself. This means I'm getting passive income through dividend payments, and those dividend payments automatically get reinvested. Also, dividend investing, to me, is fun. It allows me to push my knowledge when it comes to analyzing companies, using fundamental analysis and then buying them when they're selling at a discount.

Dividend investing also gives me confidence when it comes to investing because I'm in the driver's seat, and I'm making the decisions. It's not like when you invest in an index fund, an ETF or a mutual fund where you have a fund manager that's making all the decisions.

If you know how to analyze companies and you know how to invest in the stock market, you're less likely to get taken advantage of because you will come across people that tell you to buy specific stocks. So, you might hear friends tell you to buy specific stocks or even family members, or you might even go to a financial planner. And he's going to tell you what you need to invest in. But if you have the knowledge already because you've been investing yourself, you'll be able to pick up when people are trying to bamboozle you a lot faster.

And then the last thing besides the passive income that I generate that keeps growing within my dividend portfolio, I can also take my investment portfolio and then pass it down to, let's say, if I had kids or even pass it down to family members. And once they get it, they don't have to start from point zero because they already have an investment account that's spitting out passive income for them on a frequent basis.

In my dividend investment account, I'm enrolled in a **DRIP**. This means a dividend reinvestment plan. This means that whenever I'm getting a dividend payment from a specific company, let's say Coca-Cola, that dividend automatically gets reinvested into buying more shares of Coca-Cola. Now, this is great because you're not only getting dividend payments, but you're automatically buying more dividend-paying stocks. So, it allows you to grow your dividend income on autopilot. But one thing to remember is that even though DRIP is a good way to start when it comes to reinvesting your dividends, you still want to make sure that you're buying companies when they're selling at a discount.

You don't want to buy a company when it's overpriced. It would be better not to be enrolled into DRIP and just receive the dividend into your account, do your fundamental analysis, have those companies that you want to buy on a watch list, and then only buy them when they're selling at a discount.

But if you're just starting out, when it comes to investing in dividend-paying stocks, just go the DRIP route. So, don't worry about buying those companies that are selling at a discount with just a few dollars of dividend income. Also, not all brokerage firms allow for DRIP, so always double-check the investment firm that you're investing with to see if they allow DRIP investing.

Best Time to Buy Dividend Stocks

When is the best time to buy? I've already mentioned that you only want to buy when the company is selling at a discount. The first question, then is how can you tell if a company is selling at a discount? If a stock is trading for a dollar, does that mean that the stock is cheap? On the other hand, if a stock is trading for $1,000, does that mean that the stock is expensive? It's going to be hard to tell if you don't know what the underlying value is of that stock.

Not because the stock is trading for $1 does it mean that it's cheap. If you have a dollar in your pocket and a friend comes up to you and he wants to sell you a single piece of bubblegum, and he tells you, "You know what, I'll sell this gum to you for a dollar."

You're going to look at him like he's crazy because a single piece of bubble gum is worth less than a dollar. You could get a piece of bubble gum for $0.10. A dollar is way too overpriced! On the flip side, let's say you have $10,000 to spend and you want to buy a new car, and all of a sudden, you see that they are selling the latest model Tesla cars for $10,000. That's the steal of the century because Tesla cars are worth more than $10,000 on the market.

So, you're getting the Tesla car at a discount. That's the way you need to look at investing in dividend-paying stocks. You need to know what the value is of the stock before you go and add it to your watch list and then purchase it.

There are different ways that you can tell how much a company that's trading on the stock market is worth. Some investors like to look at, for example, the book value of a company. Other investors like to look at the earnings of a company, and then they look at the P/E ratio. The P/E ratio is a great way of trying to figure out what the company is worth, because you're looking at the net income that a company generates, also called the earnings.

If a company can increase its earnings, it also means that the company is going to be worth more. Let's say your friend has a company that generates $10,000 in net income every single year. He wants to sell it to you. So this business, let's say it's an eCommerce business, runs on autopilot generating $10k a year flat.

If he wants to sell it to you, how much are you willing to pay for it? If he wants to sell it to you for $20,000. You're buying a company for $20,000 that generates $10,000 per year. So, you'll have your invested capital back in 2 years, and any income after that is going to be pure profit. You can then take your original investment of $20,000 and invest it into a different business.

Now, let's say that another friend came up to you, and he told you that he has an eCommerce business also, but that's not doing too well. Every single month he needs to spend $4k on advertising just to get a few sales. So, he spends $4k, but he's not making any type of money, and he wants to sell this business to you for $20,000. You're not going to take that deal, because you're not going to buy a business that's hardly generating any earnings.

That's why the earnings of a company are extremely important. How much net income a company can generate, and can the company generate a net income that they can keep increasing year over year? These are the questions you should ask yourself and try to answer. On the stock market. We look at the P/E ratio, the price divided by the earnings ratio. This ratio tells you the multiple of how much you're willing to pay for the earnings of a company.

So with a P/E ratio of 15, that means that you're willing to pay 15 times the earnings of a company. In essence, that means that you will get your original capital back within 15 years. If you look at it from the earnings standpoint, I like to look at companies that have a P/E ratio of 20 or less, 15 or less is even better. That's how I decide when a company is trading at a discount or when a company is overvalued.

If we go back to the example of our friend who sold us the $10,000 generating business for $20,000. The P/E ratio would be $20k/$10k, which is a P/E ratio of 2.

When to Sell
When do I sell a dividend-paying company? I sell a company if that company changes or updates its business model into a space that they're not familiar with. For example, if a company produces chocolate chip cookies and then suddenly, they want to expand the business, and they want to jump into the technology sector, that's a big red flag because this company is used to generating income from selling chocolate chip cookies. But now they're jumping into a

whole new industry. From a financial standpoint, you can already tell that there are going to be a lot of ups and downs which might affect the dividends that they pay.

Another reason why I sell my dividend-paying stocks is when the company cuts the dividend. Anytime something bad happens economically or even if the company is going through some turmoil and it affects their net income, they might slash the dividend that they pay to their shareholders.

And then the last reason why I sell my dividend-paying stocks is if a company stops paying a dividend. There are companies that have been paying an increasing dividend year over year, but then all of a sudden, there might be an economic crash, or an economic downturn and they just stop paying a dividend. That's a big no-no because companies pride themselves on paying out dividends to their shareholders, and especially if it's a blue chip company, those companies want to keep their shareholders content, and a big way to keep their shareholders happy is by paying out a frequent dividend.

If a company pays out a dividend, but they might not increase their dividend as fast or even faster than inflation, I still hold on to the company. I bought stock in Wal-Mart, and ever since, they've been pretty much lagging with their dividend growth. However, the dividend that I do get, I just take that dividend income and invest it in another dividend-paying company.

Managing Portfolio Stocks
On average, in the US, if you buy a dividend-paying company, you get a quarterly dividend payment. Some companies might only pay twice a year. Others pay monthly. If you have a big list of companies in your portfolio, 30, 40, or 50, it's going to be harder to manage and try to figure out if you're getting dividend payments and if they are increasing, if they are staying the same, decreasing or even if one of the companies stopped paying a dividend.

The way that I do it is I export all my dividend income in an Excel spreadsheet, and then I sort the dividend income by company, month, and dividend income. This allows me to quickly see if the dividend payments that I've been getting for a specific company are increasing or not.

In the past, I had shares in Disney, but then the Disney company stopped paying dividends, and I saw that after I exported all the dividend income in my Excel spreadsheet and then sorted it and filtered it the correct way. And when I noticed that Disney was not paying a dividend anymore, I ended up selling them.

The more dividend-paying companies you have in your dividend portfolio, the harder it is going to be to manage them because it's not only about looking at the dividend-paying stocks that you have in your portfolio, but you also still need to stay up to date with them at least once a year because every year companies put out their annual report.

You want to go through the annual report and make sure that those companies are still dividend-paying companies that you want to have in your dividend portfolio. I recommend having between 20 to 30 dividend-paying companies in your portfolio. Anything over 30, and it might get a little bit harder to manage. I say 20 to 30 because it allows for diversification between your stocks.

You don't want all your eggs in one basket when it comes to investing, and when it comes to dividend investing, you don't want all your eggs in one industry basket.

Chapter 12: Best Dividend Paying Stock

I'm always careful with recommending a specific stock or company that you need to buy shares in because a company might perform well today, but that doesn't mean that the company will perform well in the future. However, the stock that I'm about to reveal is a **monthly dividend-paying stock**.

Their goal is to deliver dependable monthly dividends that increase over time. That's exactly what I want, as a value investor, from a dividend-paying company. I would add one more addition to their goal. They need to be able to deliver monthly dividends that increase over time, but that increase needs to be faster than inflation.

Luckily for you and me, this company is able to increase their dividends faster than inflation year over year, or they're able to keep up and keep pace with inflation. The company that I'm talking about is **Realty Income**. This company can also be found on the stock market under the ticker symbol **O**.

Realty Income is a company that buys commercial properties and then leases them to big-name tenants. Tenants such as Wal-Mart, CVS, Walgreens, Taco

Bell, etc. Realty Income is a REIT, also standing for Real Estate Investment Trust. Realty Income operates in the US primarily, but they also operate overseas in Europe, Spain, and the UK.

Realty Income was founded by William and Joan Clark back in 1969, and the company went public in 1994. The interesting thing about Realty Income is their business model because, from the start, Joan and William wanted to create a business that provided stable and dependable income for their shareholders. And they've been able to achieve this because not only has Realty Income been on the stock market since 1994, but they also lease to high-quality tenants. These are highly dependable tenants because even in an economic downturn, they're still able to pay their lease.

Realty Income makes sure to create lease contracts for at least ten years. There are exceptions, of course. And even if you're overseas and you go to a grocery store like Carrefour, it is more than likely Realty Income owns the property, and it's leasing it to Carrefour. And that's what I like so much about Realty Income because the dependable monthly dividends come directly from the dependable tenants.

A big benefit of Realty Income is passive income. The monthly dividend that they pay out, you can start using that as passive income. Most companies in the US pay a quarterly dividend, but with Realty Income being a monthly dividend-paying company, you can start using that as your passive income.

One of my friends that works in the IT field wants to get into making more passive income, since he's making earned income in the IT field and is making a good salary. He wants to transition slowly into making some passive income as well, and we've looked at and talked about different ways of making passive income with book publishing, creating his own YouTube channel, etc. But I keep telling him that investing in dividend-paying companies, that's the easiest way to start building your passive income. And with Realty Income paying a monthly dividend, that's a great way to start your passive income journey.

Realty Income has been able to increase its dividend 114 times. They've been paying a dividend since 1994, and there wasn't a dividend decrease since 1999. So that's over 20 years of dividend payments, which shows their consistency and dependability. That's the type of company that I like because you invest in the company once, and you reap the benefits. And this allows you to sleep well at night because even if overall the stock market isn't performing well, you can still hold on to your Realty Income shares and still get that dividend because most companies in the US pay a quarterly dividend, so every three months you see a dividend payment being deposited into your account.

And then, if you look at companies overseas, it's not that consistent depending on the company when they pay out a dividend. Also, they might not even grow their dividends faster than inflation. That's why with this monthly dividend-paying company, you're in good hands.

For my portfolio, I use Realty Income as my foundation, and any additional dividend stocks that I buy are sitting on top of my foundation. What it will look like is that whenever Realty Income increases its dividends, it increases my overall foundation, and then the other dividend payments sit on top. If you look at your dividend payments month by month, you'll see that your income will swing up and down because different companies pay their dividends in different months.

But with Realty Income being the stable monthly dividend-paying company, that's why I use them as my foundation. I've been invested in Realty Income for a couple of years now. So, I've been getting my monthly dividends for a few years on time, every single month, around the middle of the month, and I've been buying additional shares. When I get my dividend, I either reinvest it into buying more shares in Realty Income, or I take that dividend, and I invest into other dividend-paying companies.

Another thing that I like about Realty Income is its corporate responsibility. With any company that I invest in, as a value investor, I like to look at a company that generates a healthy amount of net income that can grow year over year, because if they can do that, more than likely, they're also going to be able to increase the dividends that they pay out to shareholders year over year. I also like to look at a company's business model, and I like to see what type of business this company is engaged in, because there might be some business models that you don't agree with.

There might be specific companies that you don't like to invest in which are in specific industries. Luckily for us, Realty Income has a safe and stable business model. Also, the Realty Income Management team has been doing a great job of managing the business, but then also growing the company by expanding overseas.

I'm pretty sure that they're also looking at other countries to expand into because currently, they have close to 12,000 commercial properties that they own. Since they've been in the business since 1969, they've been able to develop a plan and a system that's plug-and-play, so they know what to look for. They know how to analyze specific properties, and specific locations, and all they have to do is plug their system in a specific location, and we, the shareholders, reap the reward from it.

When deciding when to buy a Real Estate Investment trust or REIT, such as Realty Income, you cannot use the P/E ratio. What you need to do is you need to take the E, which is the earnings, and substitute that with the FFO, the **funds from operations**. The funds from operations measures the performance of your Real Estate Investment Trust.

What you need to do is take the P divided by the AFFO, which is the adjusted funds from operations, that's going to tell you if your company is selling at a discount or not. I'm looking at the AFFO from the annual report that Realty Income gave. And in 2021, it was at $3.59. Currently, the stock is trading at around $64. $64 divided by $3.59 is 17.8. I'd like to see that below 15. But 17 to 18, that's a good ratio also.

Chapter 13: Investing in your 20s vs 50s

Why would you even think about investing when you're young? Because you still have your whole life ahead of you. You're not thinking about investing. You're not thinking about retirement. You just want to live your life and have fun. You might want to buy the latest video games or even the newest sneakers. And you might also be scared to start investing because you don't know where to start.

The investing world is big and confusing, and you might need some help. However, when you start thinking about retirement, the younger you are when you start planning for your retirement, the easier it's going to be to hit your retirement goal.

For example, when I was in my early twenties, I worked at a retail store, and this was one of the first jobs that I had. This company that I worked at had a 401k representative come through to talk about retirement and had employees ask questions about their 401k, their retirement, and any other miscellaneous questions they might have.

I went into that meeting, and looked around and I noticed that I was the only young person in that whole meeting. I was in my early twenties and everybody else was in their mid to late fifties and up, which surprised me because even at a young age, I was already thinking about what I needed to do in order to be able to put myself in a position where I'm already financially free, and I would be able to retire early and just live the life that I want to live.

That was my whole mindset. But all the young people that I worked with did not have that same mindset. They were focused on buying the latest materialistic things such as headphones, new iPhones, and the list goes on. So, if you're already thinking about retirement at a young age, you're way ahead of your peers!

The employees that were in their fifties at the meeting felt defeated because they felt that it was too late for them to start investing for retirement. But even at that age, you can still catch up. It's going to take more effort, but you can still work on your retirement. Everyone's investing journey is going to be different, but if you're younger, when you start to invest, you'll be able to take more risks.

You'll be able to invest in equities or even securities such as stocks that have historically been able to provide a better rate of return than fixed-income assets like bonds. When you're young, you can invest 80%, maybe even 90% in stocks, but the older you get and when you start hitting your fifties, you want to make that switch and start to invest in more fixed-income assets such as bonds, annuities, and some dividend-paying stocks.

Even when you're older, above 50 or 60, you still need to have a portion of your investment portfolio in stocks because you still want that rate of return that stocks can give you compared to fixed-income assets.

The biggest benefit that you have when you start investing at a young age is that you have a long timeline to build and grow your wealth. Because if you start investing at a young age, your money can compound for you. So, the money that you invest, even if you start out by investing a small amount of money on a frequent basis, that money can compound.

And when it comes to your capital compounding in the stock market. There are three ways this happens. It happens with capital gains, interest, and dividends. With capital gains, any money that you've invested in the stock market has the potential to gain in value, which is also called an unrealized capital gain. Now, the second one is interest. So, if you invest in a fixed-income asset such as a bond, you'll get interest payments on a frequent basis. And then the last one, dividend payments. Dividends that you do get from dividend-paying companies, are going to be reinvested in order to buy more shares of stock. Those three methods of compounding your money in the stock market are going to make it possible for you to invest a little bit of money, which will make your money compound and allow you to build wealth.

If you graduated from college and started working and you have already invested, let's say, $2,000 in a 401k. And the company that you work at also gives you an employer match. You have $2,000 invested at the age of 24, and then every single month, you invest $1,000, which is doable with an employer match. When you hit the age of 50, you'll be a millionaire. If you can get a rate of return of around 8%, inflation not accounted for.

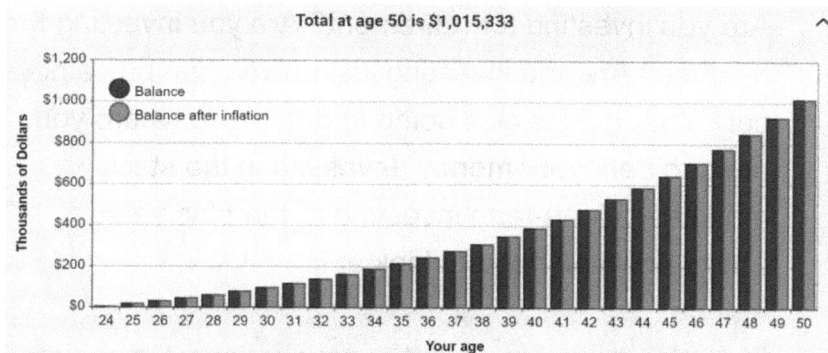

Total at age 50 is $1,015,333

Now, if you're at the age of 40 and you still want to be a millionaire by age 50, if you take the same metrics by looking at a rate of return of 8% and if you have $2,000 invested in your 401k, you will have to invest close to $5,500 a month just to be a millionaire by age 50. Starting at 24 allows you to invest significantly less because your money compounds over time. But if you start investing at a later age, you're going to have to catch up. In your situation, you might not start to invest at the age of 24, and you might not even have close to $1,000 to invest every single month. Everybody's situation is going to be different. But one thing that is important is that you have an investing goal because when you start investing, you don't just want to invest just for the sake of investing. You do need to have a goal.

145

Are you investing for retirement? Are you investing for a house? Are you investing just so you can buy a new car? Your goal is also going to determine where you need to park your money. Investing in the stock market is a long-term investment, ten-plus years. That's how you need to look at it.

But let's say you just want to save up some money for a car or even for a down payment on a house. There are other financial vehicles out there that you can use. It might just be better to put the money that you are saving to buy a car in a savings account, a money market account or a certificate of deposit.

But with investing, try to stay away from the mindset of thinking that it should happen fast because investing is a steady process. It is doable to become a 401k millionaire. You would just have to run the numbers in order to figure out how much you need to invest in order to become a 401k millionaire.

The stock market is not predictable, but you can look at historical data and look at the rate of return over the years to figure out and plot how much you need to invest and how long it will take you to become a millionaire when it comes to investing in the stock market.

If you are younger, it is more than likely you don't have the knowledge when it comes to investing in different types of securities. This knowledge comes with time, experience, and making mistakes. It's something that you need to take in stride and something that you need to learn from. Look at your failures not as mistakes but as a part of the learning process. If you're younger, you might have some free time to try day trading or even options trading. But when you're older, you might not want to participate in high-risk, high-reward ways of trying to make money in the stock market. Especially when you're older, and you're close to retirement age, or you're already retired, you don't want to stress over your capital or your money and the value of it going up and down. You want a steady stream of income that you can rely on. So fixed income assets will play a major role.

Even if you can do anything outside of the stock market, for example, if you own rental properties through real estate or even if you have a business that provides you with a stable, consistent income every month, that's what you can also be building towards in your younger years.

Investing in Crypto

Investing in the stock market is still going to be your best option. But in the world that we live in now, especially with crypto, I can also see crypto playing a major role in the future in how people construct their portfolios. Currently, you might have some stocks, some bonds, and you might even have some commodities. But going into the future, I can also see people and even companies adding more currencies like crypto ETF investments into investment portfolios.

Anything that you do when it comes to investing involves risk, especially in the crypto market. So crypto will be something that you need to pay even more attention to as it's a lot more volatile than even some of the stocks that you can purchase in the stock market that I discussed earlier. If you're a lazy investor, if you're more of a set-it-and-forget-it type of investor, you don't want to log in and constantly pay attention to how your stocks are performing or how your index fund, ETF or mutual funds are performing and if you work at a company that also offers a 401k, more than likely you can invest in a **target date fund**.

Some target date funds, once they hit that retirement age, stop rebalancing, but there are some target date funds that still rebalance the portfolio after retirement age. Make sure to double-check the target date fund that you're investing in to see if it's one that does rebalance after the retirement age or if it doesn't.

For this privilege of laziness, because you just invest in a target date fund and you don't have to touch it because everything is being done for you, for this privilege, you can expect a higher expense ratio because there is a fund manager that actively rebalances the target date fund, which you will be paying for. Also, if you want to invest in a target date fund, make sure that that's 100% of your investment portfolio because if you're going to be introducing other securities besides that target date fund, you're going to mess up your asset allocation. Your asset allocation shows you how much money or the percentage of money is allocated to a specific investment, whether it might be stocks, bonds, crypto commodities, art, etc.

When to Start Investing

There's no right or wrong age when it comes to investing, but the sooner, the better because as I mentioned earlier, if you start investing at a young age, you have all that time for your money to compound and build your wealth. You don't want to put off investing because before you know it, months will go by, years, even potentially decades. And you'll be wondering where all that time went.

When you start investing at a young age, a good way to look at it is that you will be able to make time work in your favor because the older we get, the faster time seems to be going. However, if you're older, you might be saying to yourself, I'm way too old to start investing.

You're never too old to start investing. Because if there's a company that you work at and that company offers a 401k, you have a higher contribution limit if you're above the age of 50. Also called the catch-up contribution. This allows you to invest even more than the current limit just to catch up and allow you to grow your investments potentially at a faster rate.

Custodial Account
If you're very young, you might be under the age of 15, but you still want to invest. What you need is a custodial account set up for you. A custodial account can be set up by your parents or an adult supervisor. They're able to open a custodial account with any of the big-name investment firms. Once you have that custodial account set up, always invest with your parent or your legal guardian because when you are

at a young age, you do want adult supervision when it comes to investing.

If you're an older investor or an investor that's already retired, you might be invested in dividend-paying stocks. But if you're a young investor, it's ok to invest in dividend-paying stocks even if these dividend-paying stocks don't grow as fast as, let's say, a growth stock which has a higher rate of return. Even for a younger investor, be sure to invest in dividend-paying stocks because if you're young and you're just starting out investing, it's not always about seeing how much money you can make.

It's also a learning process, and you want to know the ins and outs of some of the securities that are available to you. What you want to do is not put all your eggs in one basket. So don't put all your investment money in dividend-paying stocks, but make sure that you do have a few dividend-paying stocks or even a dividend index fund or dividend ETF in your portfolio.

And if you happen to find out that you do like dividend investing, then you can always take it to the next level and start doing some fundamental analysis in order to analyze dividend-paying companies like a value investor would do it. The mindset is what I want you to keep in mind in order to start investing at a young age, and invest any amount that you can, even if it's a couple of dollars here or there because your money will compound.

Chapter 14: 8 Investing Mistakes That Will Leave You Broke

There's a lot of investing misinformation, and I'm here to dispel it. Some of these mistakes I've made myself, or I might know friends or family members that made some of these mistakes. Hopefully, you will learn from our mistakes.

The first thing you must be careful of are the investing gurus. You always want to be careful of people talking to you and giving you advice on what type of stocks you need to invest in because the biggest issue that I have with these investing gurus is that they will tell you when you should buy a specific stock, but they never tell you when to sell that stock. Not everybody that's giving you investing advice has bad intentions, of course, because some people just like investing. They get hyped up when it comes to companies that they like.

So, they might like Tesla, Google or Facebook. Out of their good nature. They might tell you to go ahead and invest in Tesla. But you must always pay attention to investing gurus that have a financial component to the advice that they give because there are a lot of gurus that get a kickback or commission if they promote a specific stock or company. So always do your research on who's giving you this advice. Is it coming from a person on the television, or is it coming from somebody on the Internet? Always do a little bit of digging to see if there are any financial incentives tied to the advice that this person is actually giving you.

The second mistake is investing without doing your research. So, this goes hand in hand with the guru because the guru will jump up and tell you what to invest in. You don't do your own research, and you just jump and invest in that stock or mutual fund.

This is a quick way to invest in companies that might be worthless. Nowadays, it's extremely easy to do research on a company because all this information is available online. All you need is the company's name or even the ticker symbol. You can search Google and start reading what the company does, how much the company is generating in revenue, sales, net income, how much debt the company actually has, etc.

Don't just buy something on a hunch, and even if you want to be on the safe side, you can always invest in an ETF or an index fund that tracks an underlying index.

The third one is thinking that it's too late to start investing. Sometimes I talk to people that are older, 50 and up, and they've never invested in the stock market. They tell me it's too late for them to start investing. But the way I always look at it is that you won't be able to work your whole life. There will come a time when you're physically not able to work, and in that case, you will need to have money available that you've generated over all those years and decades. You need to have that money working for you. So even if you think that it's too late to start investing, you still need to dip your toe into the investing swimming pool because it's not only about you, it's also about your next of kin, which might be your nephews, your nieces, your kids, even other family members that you can pass your investments down to.

And even if you're scared to start investing, you can always start by investing a little bit of money. Nobody tells you that you need to start investing thousands of dollars. You can start small. You don't even need to buy a whole share. You can buy a fraction of a share. So even if you have $50, $100, or $200, just start where you are. And when you do get more comfortable, that's when you can add more money to invest in different stocks, bonds, ETFs, mutual funds, etc. And when you invest a small amount, it's a lot less stressful, and it's also going to be a lot more fun. You learn the basics, and before you know it, you'll be adding more money to invest or better yet, you can dollar cost average.

And that brings me to the next one, being too afraid to invest in the stock market because people always hear horror stories, so they might know a friend or even a family member that put all of their money in a specific stock. That company ended up going bankrupt, and they lost all their money. The problem with this is that not investing in the stock market might be a big reason why you will go broke. The money that you have might be in a savings account or even a checking account. But the money that you have in those accounts will not grow faster than inflation.

When you invest in stocks or even bonds, at least your money is able to keep pace with inflation or grow faster than inflation. So, your money retains its buying power. But if you earn your money and you put it under your mattress or put it in a savings account, which gives you less than 1% in interest, your money is going to be worth less over time. In this situation, your money is losing its buying power over time, and you're more than likely not able to work in your elder years, that's going to leave you broke pretty fast.

The following mistake is being too emotional. When you invest, it's easy to get hyped up when you see the stock market in a bull run, which means, on average, the stock market is going up. And it's also fun to see your favorite stocks going up over time. But what happens when a stock crashes or a stock dips down? Are you going to be emotionally sound enough to still hold on to your stock, or are you going to panic and sell your stocks? That's something that you will also have to learn. If you start investing with a small amount of money, you will see the value of your investments go up and down. But since you started with a small amount, it's not going to hit you that hard. It's only when you have thousands of dollars and even hundreds of thousands of dollars invested in the stock market and you see the stock market dip or crash by 30% or more. Are you going to get emotional then and start selling like crazy? That's something that you don't want to do on a hunch.

Even if everybody around you starts selling, you still want to take a step back, take a deep breath, and really think about what you're about to do, more than likely the stock market or the stocks, after investing in, especially if you're investing in an index fund or an ETF, more than likely it will bounce back.

It might take some time; it might take months or even years for it to bounce back. But at least you're not losing your money because the money is still invested in the stock market. So, the loss that you're seeing is an unrealized loss. It only becomes a realized loss if you sell that particular security.

Mistake number six is falling for a pump and dump. This kind of thing goes back to the gurus I talked about earlier. So, you will have somebody that advertises or tells you that you should buy a specific stock or specific security. They might not only tell you, but they have a whole audience that they are advertising to buy that specific stock. Everybody ends up buying that stock, in essence, increasing the value and the price of the stock, in other words, pumping up the price of the stock. And when the price is at its highest, that's when these unscrupulous gurus sell all their stocks in that specific company, and they make a quick profit.

Meanwhile, since they're selling, the stock price will going down and cause it to crash and you're pretty much ending up with a stock that is worth nothing. This is the dumping of the stock. So, you just got scammed by the pump-and-dump method.

The funny thing is that my dad actually got scammed with a pump-and-dump. This happened back in 2004 or 2005. He got a phone call from an investment firm which was pitching him a specific stock or a group of stocks to invest in. I was not listening to that phone call because I was not with my dad. But what ended up happening was that he invested in that specific security, and within a couple of months, its value of it tanked so much that it was worth nothing. That experience turned him off from investing for a long time.

It wasn't until I started investing and teaching him some of the things to look out for that he got back into investing. He never told me this story, he only told my brother, and if he had told me the story when it happened, I might have also refrained from investing in the stock market. Luckily, I never went that route.

Mistake number seven is putting your money into just one or two stocks. It's easy to get excited about specific stocks or just put all your money in one specific stock.

But that's the riskiest thing you can do because you don't want to put all your eggs in one basket. You want to spread your money across a multitude of stocks, bonds, and even securities. It allows you to lower your risk because if all your money is invested in one stock and that company goes bankrupt, you pretty much lose all your money. But if your money is spread out over ten or more securities, even if one ends up crashing or you lose money in one, you still have a good chunk of money invested in the other securities.

This also puts your mind at ease. It will also make you sleep well at night because you're not only focusing on one stock or investment since it's spread out over so many. A good way to diversify without even having to think about it is to buy a high-quality ETF or index fund. Anything that tracks the S&P 500 is also a good start. The Vanguard Company has a lot of good ETFs and index funds that you can invest in. This will give you instant diversification.

Number eight is timing the market vs time in the market. There's nothing wrong with trying to time the market, and I know day traders and swing traders that are experts at knowing when to buy and sell.

However, even they themselves take losses. If you're just a beginner who's investing or you're just a novice, timing the market will more than likely not work for you.

It's better to just buy and hold. And over the long run, you will see your investment grow. Most people that jump into the stock market think that they can get rich fast, but investing shouldn't be looked at like that.

For every one story that you hear of somebody getting rich fast in the stock market, there are millions of others that actually ended up losing their shirt. So, look at investing as a slower process of building wealth and getting rich.

Chapter 15: 5 Tips to Get Rich in the Stock Market

You have all these different avenues that you can use to make money, such as real estate or even crypto. But the stock market is still one of the best options and one of the easiest options to start building your wealth.

The first step is setting a goal because it's extremely easy to just start investing without having a goal because that's how I started investing. I just started spending money buying different shares, and buying different stocks. I had no specific goal. I just jumped in because I wanted to learn how the stock market worked. But after purchasing a few shares of stock, I quickly noticed that I needed to have a specific goal when I'm investing in the stock market.

If you think about a goal, a goal is nothing more than a roadmap to success. If you get out of the house and you take a taxi, your taxicab is going to want to know where he or she is supposed to take you. If you tell them that you want to go downtown. Your taxi driver has a clear goal. They have a specific location that they need to go to.

After you've set up your goal, you need to know the steps that you need to take in order to achieve that goal. If you have a goal of having $1,000,000 or even a $2 million investment account. That's your goal. If you want to hit that goal by age 40. The next step is to plan out your goal, so you can plan out the years that you still have in order to achieve your million to $2 million investment account. And you can also figure out what your rate of return needs to be on average every single year to hit your goal.

And then you can also figure out how much you need to invest on a frequent basis using dollar cost averaging to hit that specific goal. Setting a goal is of the utmost importance.

Tip number two on how to get rich by making money in the stock market is that you need to start investing in securities that can help you grow your wealth fast. Investing in the stock market has a lot of risks associated with it. How stocks performed in the past might not be an excellent indicator of how those stocks will perform in the future. But that's something that we have to look at. We can look at how stocks, ETFs, index funds or even mutual funds have performed in the past. And based on that performance, try to predict how it will perform in the future. If you want to grow your wealth fast in the stock market, a good place to start is by investing in ETFs. The reason why you want to invest in ETFs is because they are a passive way of investing. So, you don't have to do all the fundamental analysis to make sure that you're investing in the right stocks or even the right fixed-income assets. With an ETF, you get diversification depending on the ETF that you purchase.

Tip number three, make sure that you're investing in tax-efficient accounts. Nothing is worse than investing your hard-earned money, seeing it grow and then having to pay a boatload of taxes on your wealth. That's why you must pay attention to which accounts you open and invest in. If, for example, you look at a traditional 401k, you invest with pre-tax money, so you invest your money before taxes are taken out, and your money can grow.

And tip number four is having the right mindset when it comes to investing. And the right mindset when it comes to investing is all about consistency. Everybody nowadays has shiny object syndrome, which means people are scatterbrained. One day they want to invest in the stock market, then the next day, they hear about crypto and then the following day, they want to do real estate. When it comes to the right mindset, you just want to focus on investing consistently, making sure that you have that goal, and then executing until you hit your goal.

Having the right mindset when it comes to investing, it's not something fun. It's not something sexy. It's boring, but boring and consistency will lead to you becoming rich and building your wealth.

The last tip, number five, has to do with outside-of-the-box thinking. You need to start investing for your kids or any family members that are growing up now. How awesome would it be if your parents or even your grandparents already had an investment account set up for you? And then, when you're of age, you take ownership of that account, and you just continue the investing process.

Even when I look at my little niece and my little cousin, I went ahead, and bought them their first share of stock both in Coca-Cola and Disney, which will get them thinking about investing. I'm investing for them right now, and then when they're old enough, when they are both adults, they'll be able to take ownership of their investments. This is also a great way of getting kids involved in the stock market because school is not going to teach them how to invest.

More than likely, their friends are not going to tell them the best way to start investing. It needs to come from somebody just like yourself who's interested in investing and is currently actually working on buying investments, buying ETFs, mutual funds, index funds, and working on building your wealth.

The knowledge that you do gain along the way. That's the knowledge that you can pass down. And even if you do not want to go the route of buying individual shares of stock, you can always open a custodial account and be the legal guardian and the adult supervisor of that custodial account.

Conclusion

If you've made it all the way to the end, I need to give you a round of applause because it means that you are serious about your investing journey.

Keep in mind that investing might not always be glamorous, and you might even get frustrated or stressed out, but it's all about having the fortitude to stick to your goal and press forward. There will be a lot of ups and downs in the stock market, but if you're emotionally sound, you'll be able to easily weather the storm.

I covered a lot of information, so feel free to go back if there is anything that you want to review or if there is a specific stock or ETF that I mentioned before that you want to do more research on.

If each of us can influence just one person to take their financial life and retirement more seriously, I feel like I would have accomplished my goal :)

www.ingramcontent.com/pod-product-compliance
Lightning Source LLC
Chambersburg PA
CBHW071644210326
41597CB00017B/2108